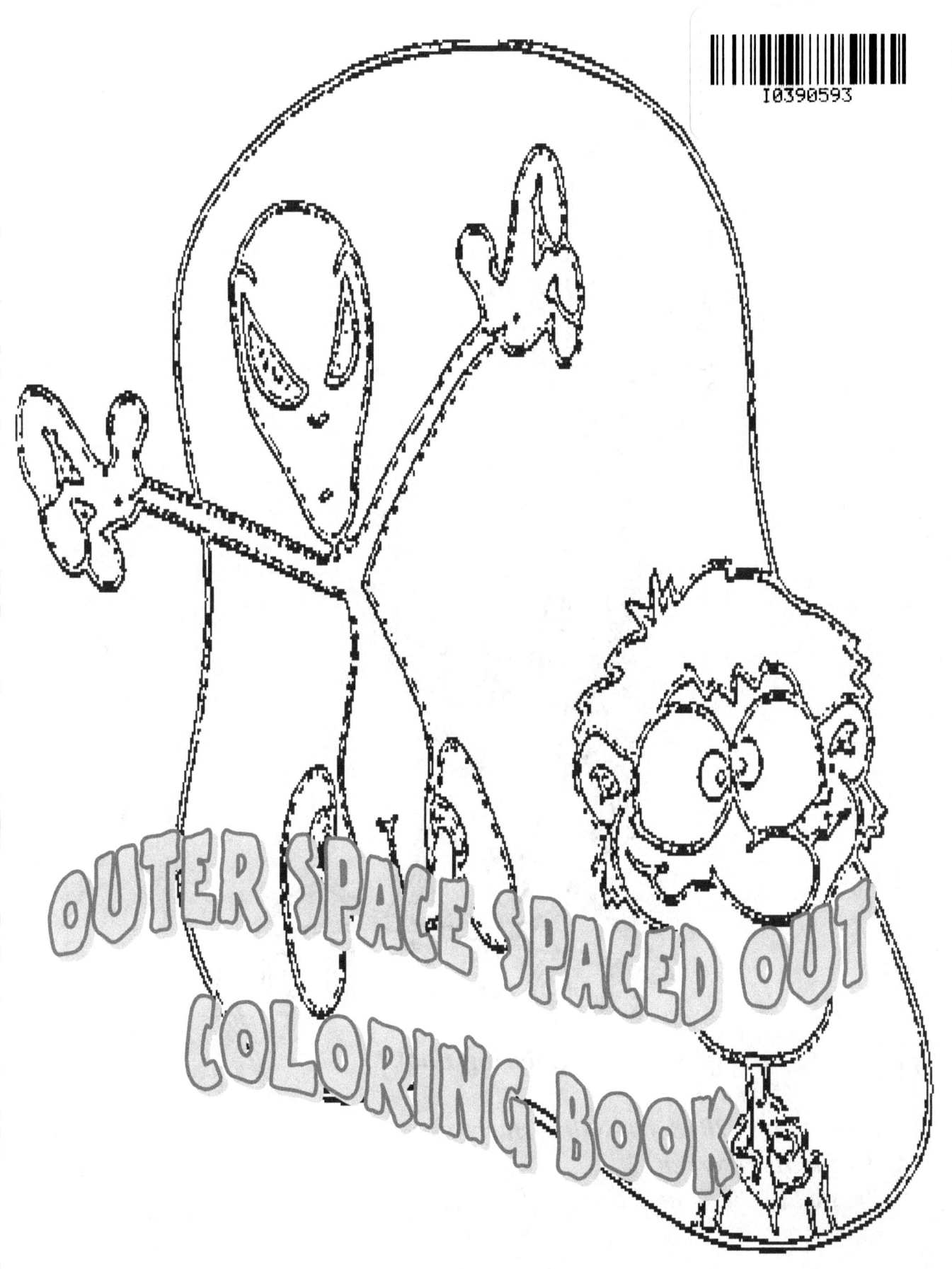

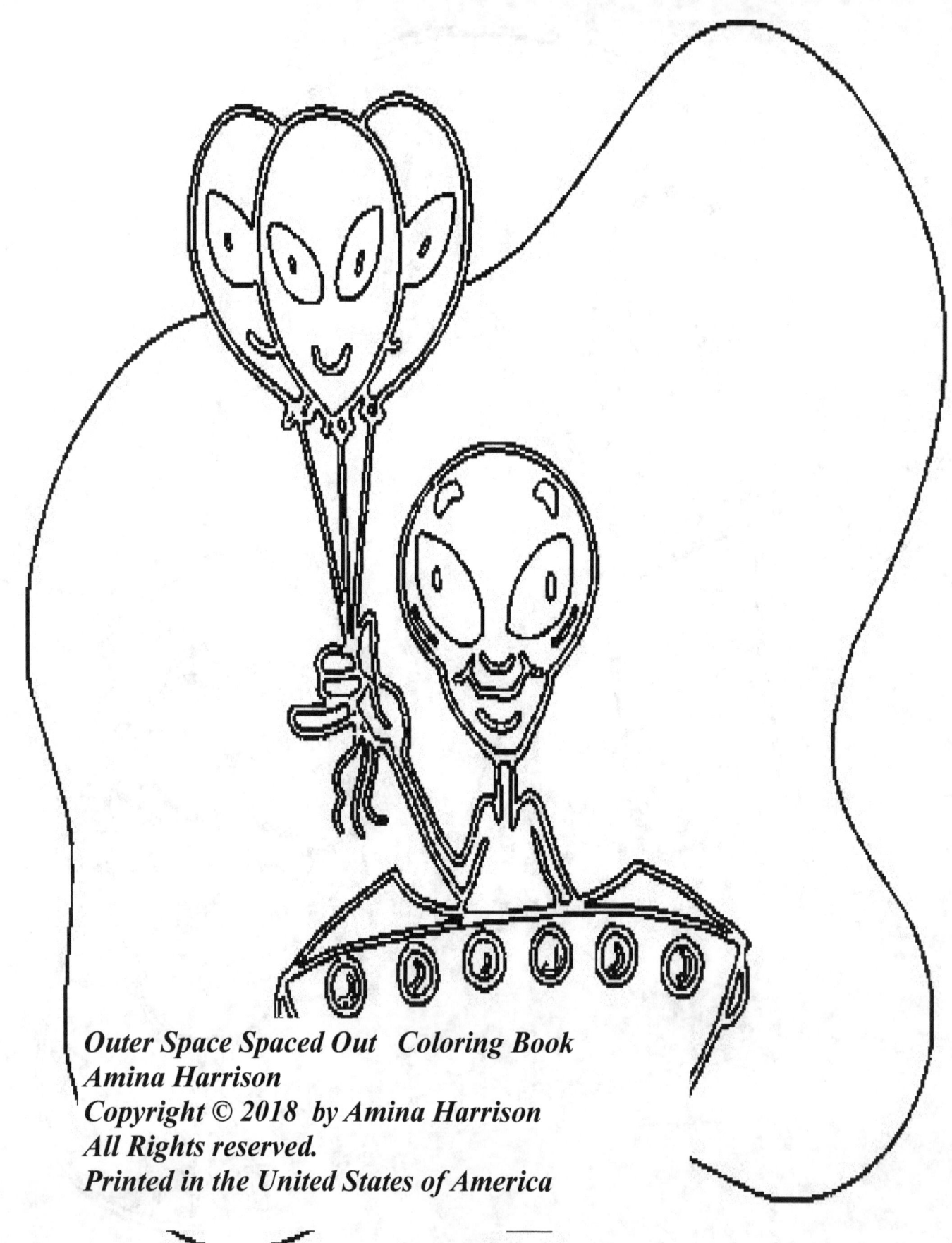

Outer Space Spaced Out   Coloring Book
Amina Harrison
Copyright © 2018 by Amina Harrison
All Rights reserved.
Printed in the United States of America

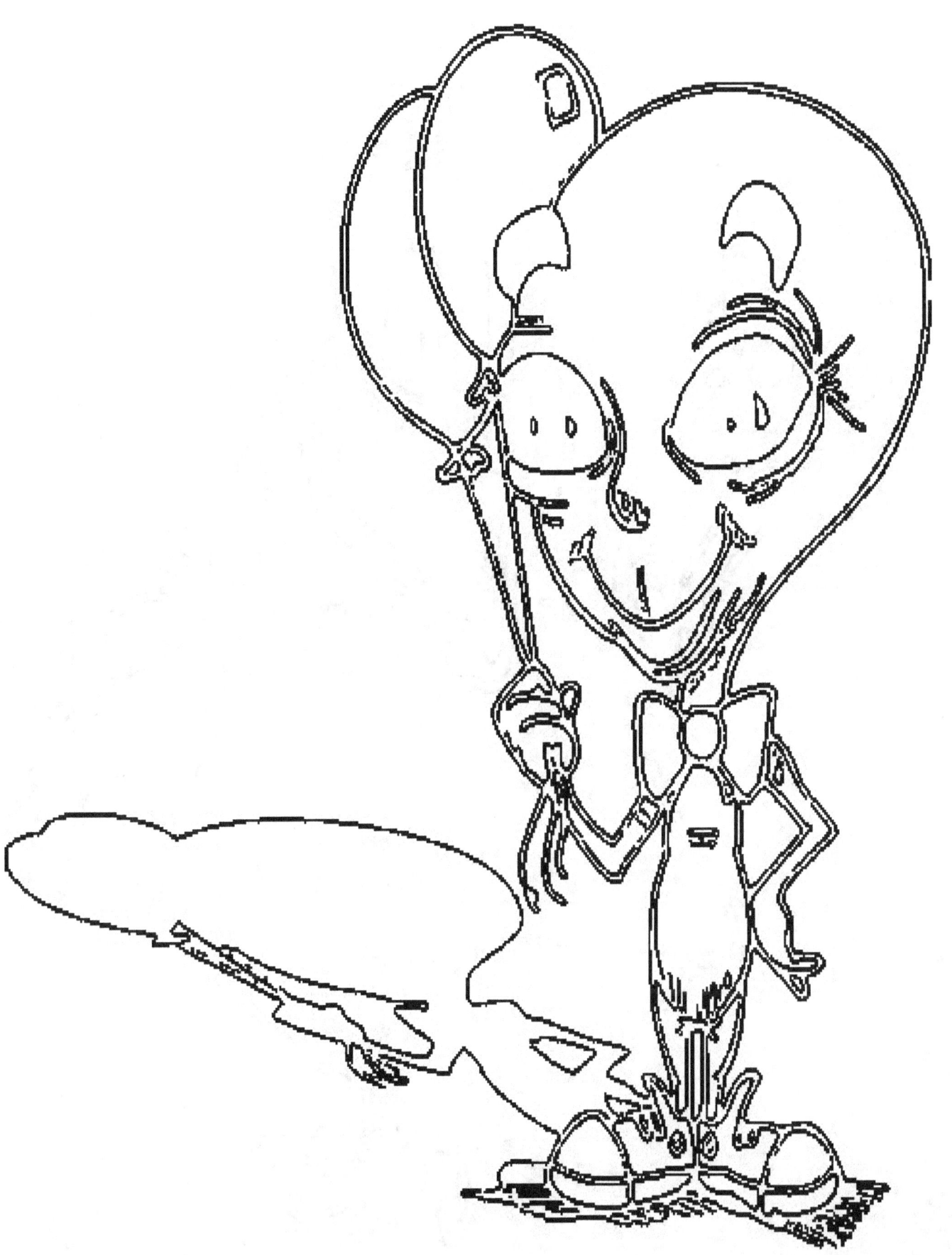

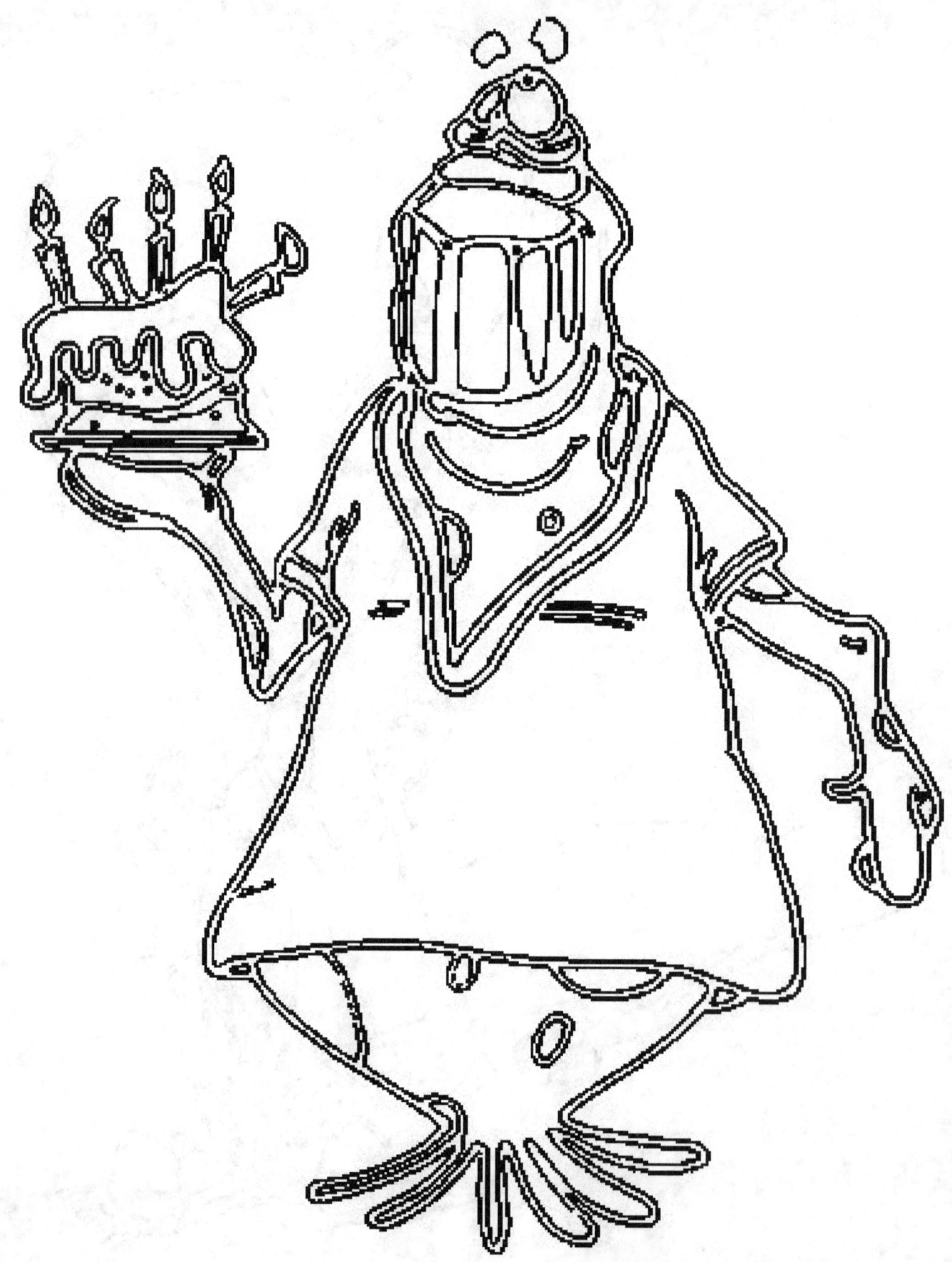

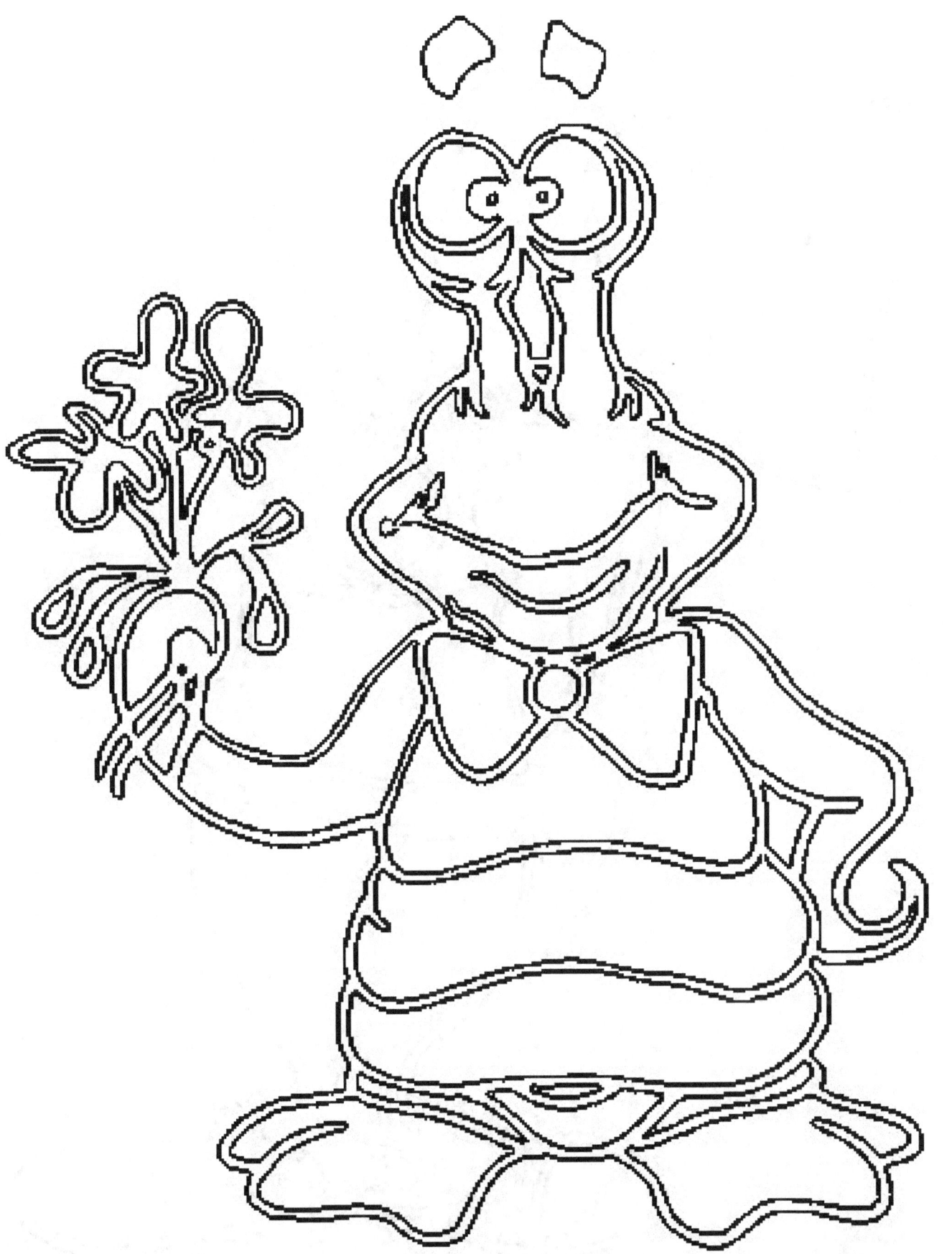

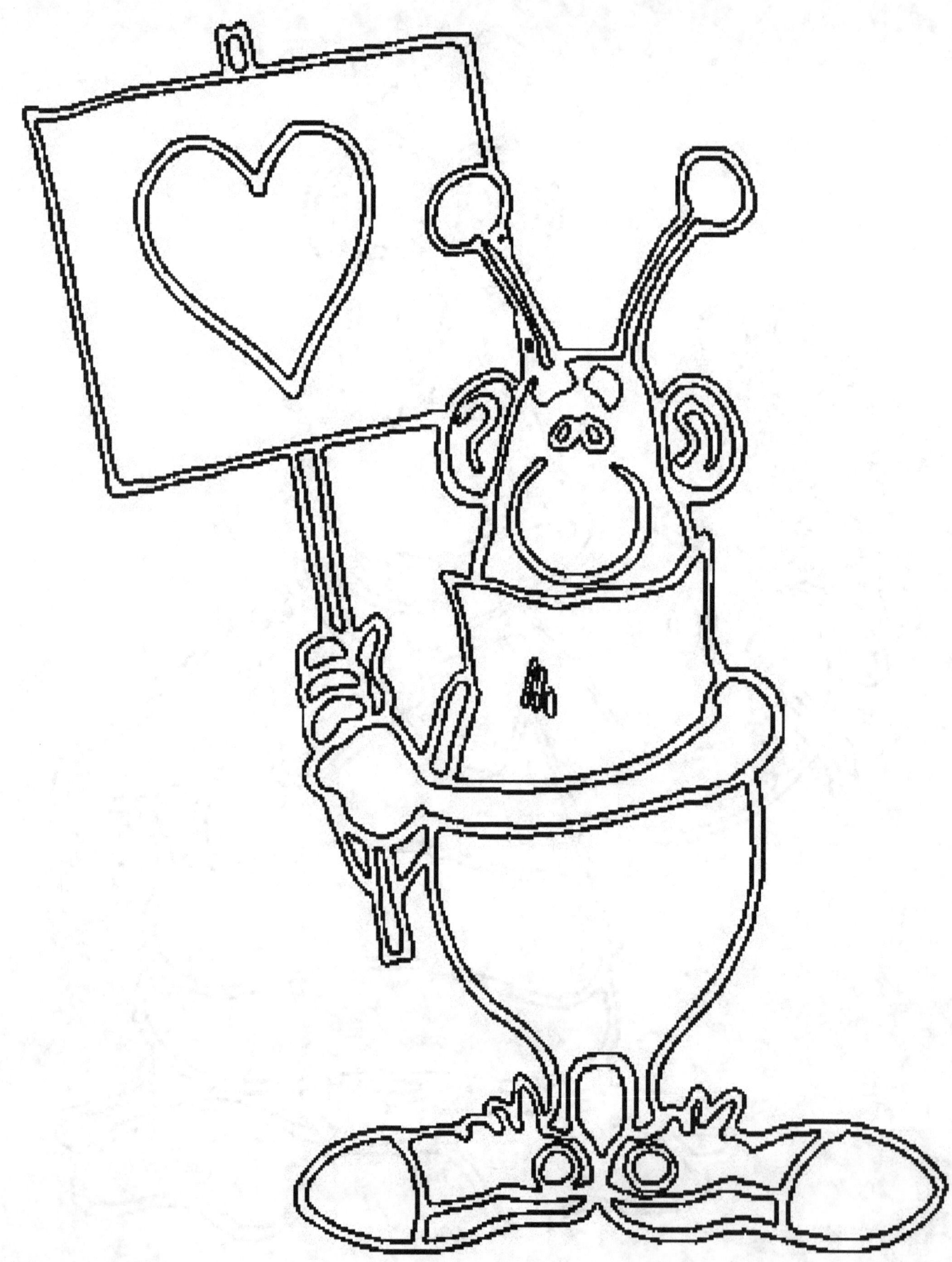

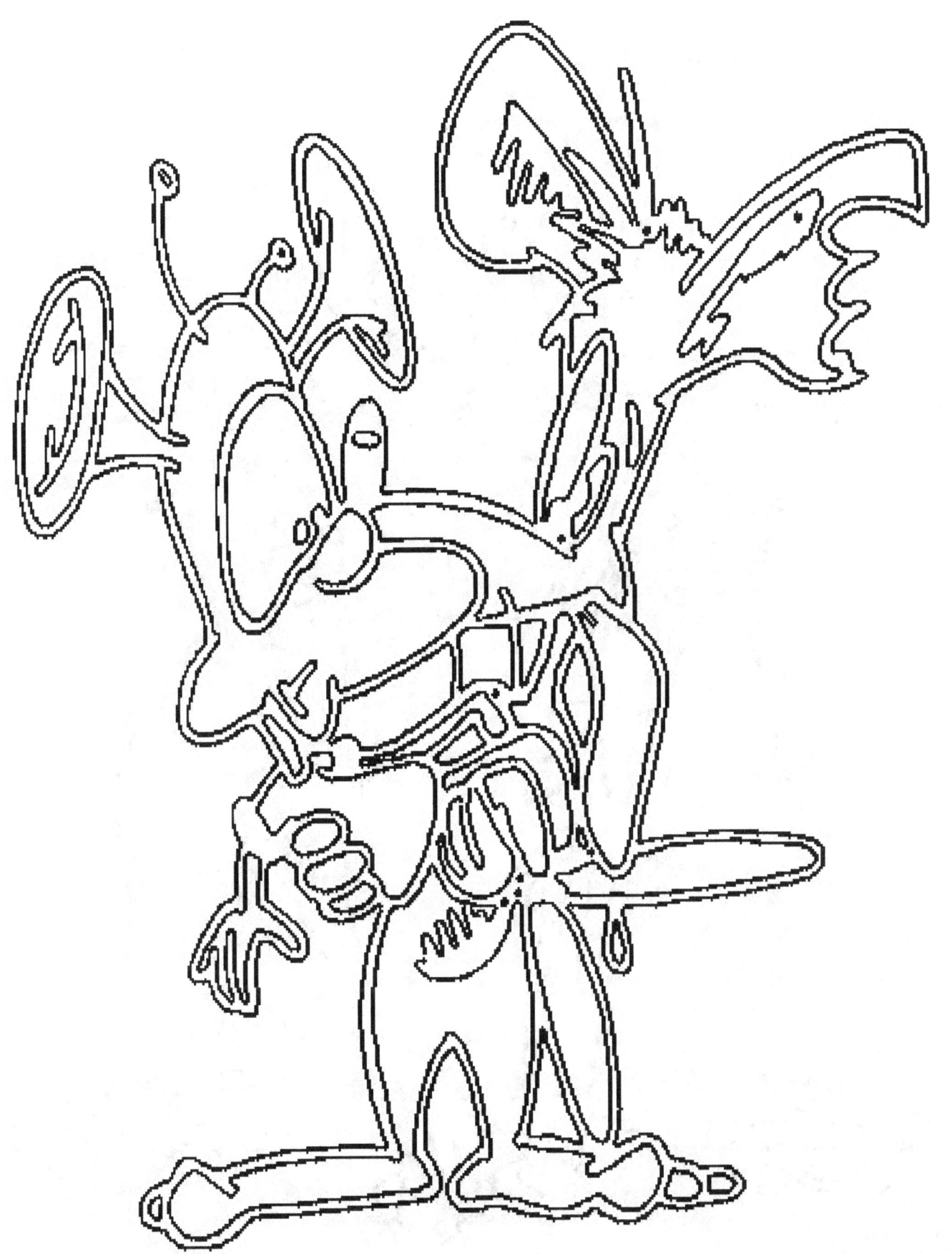

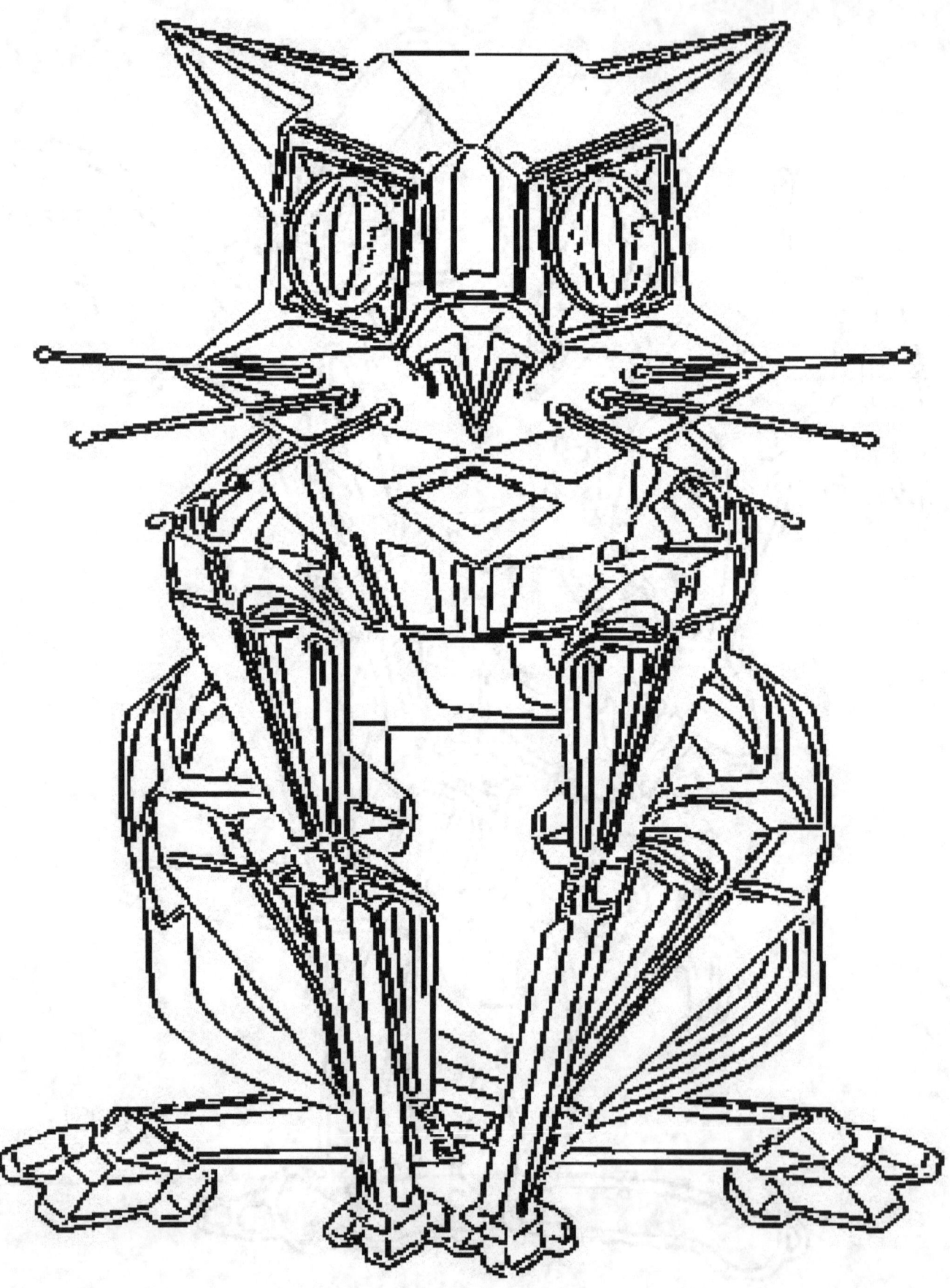

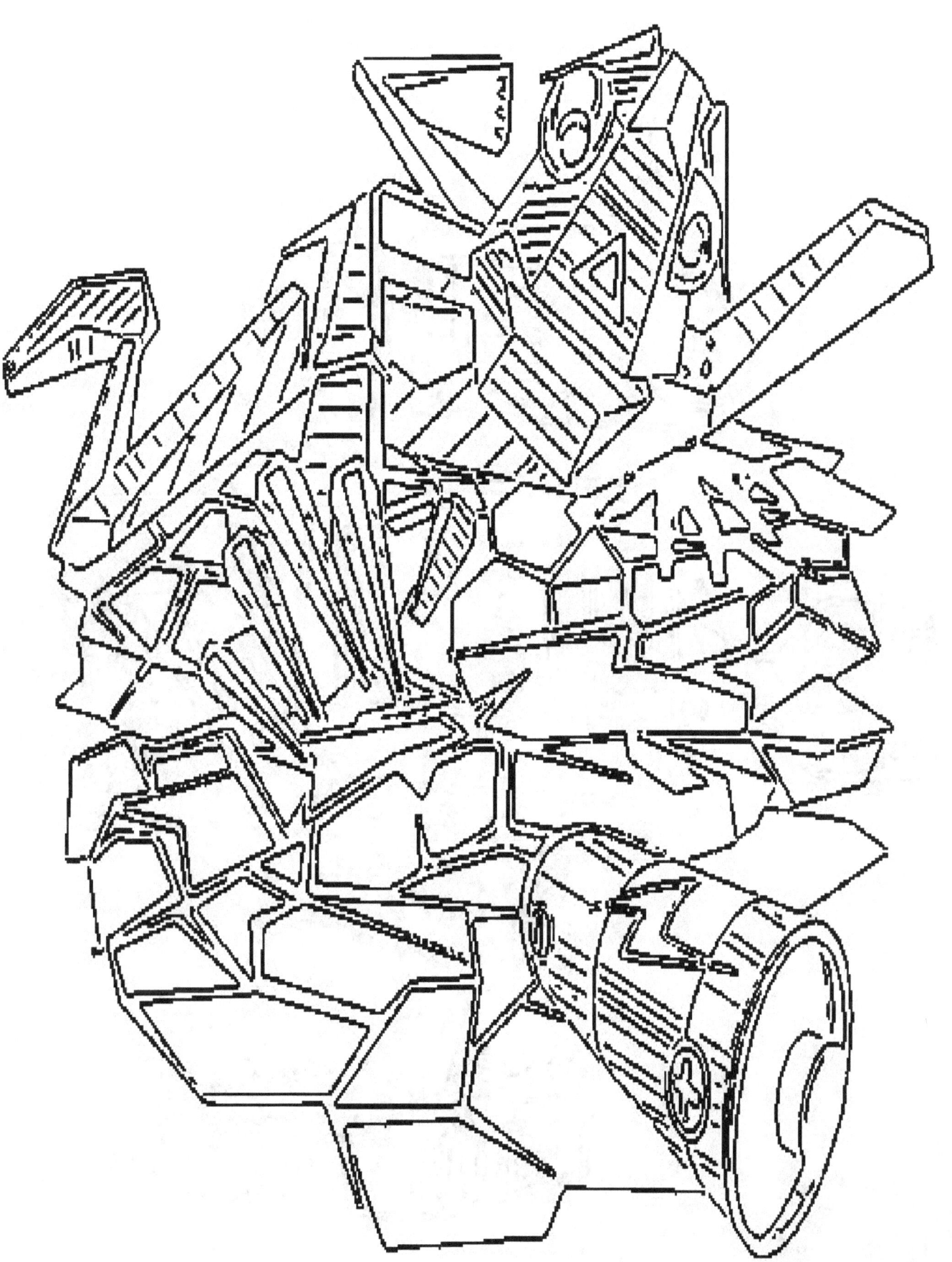

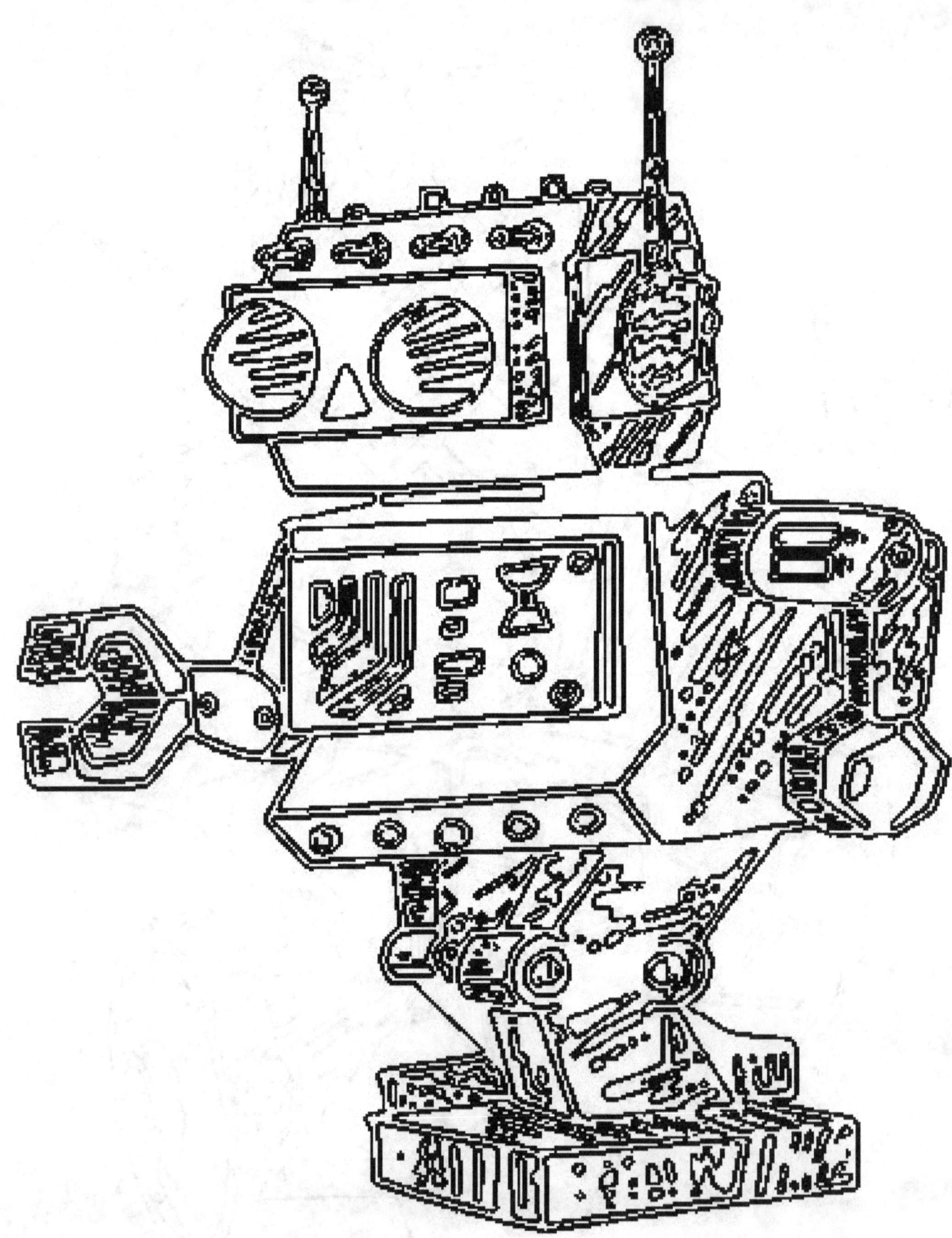

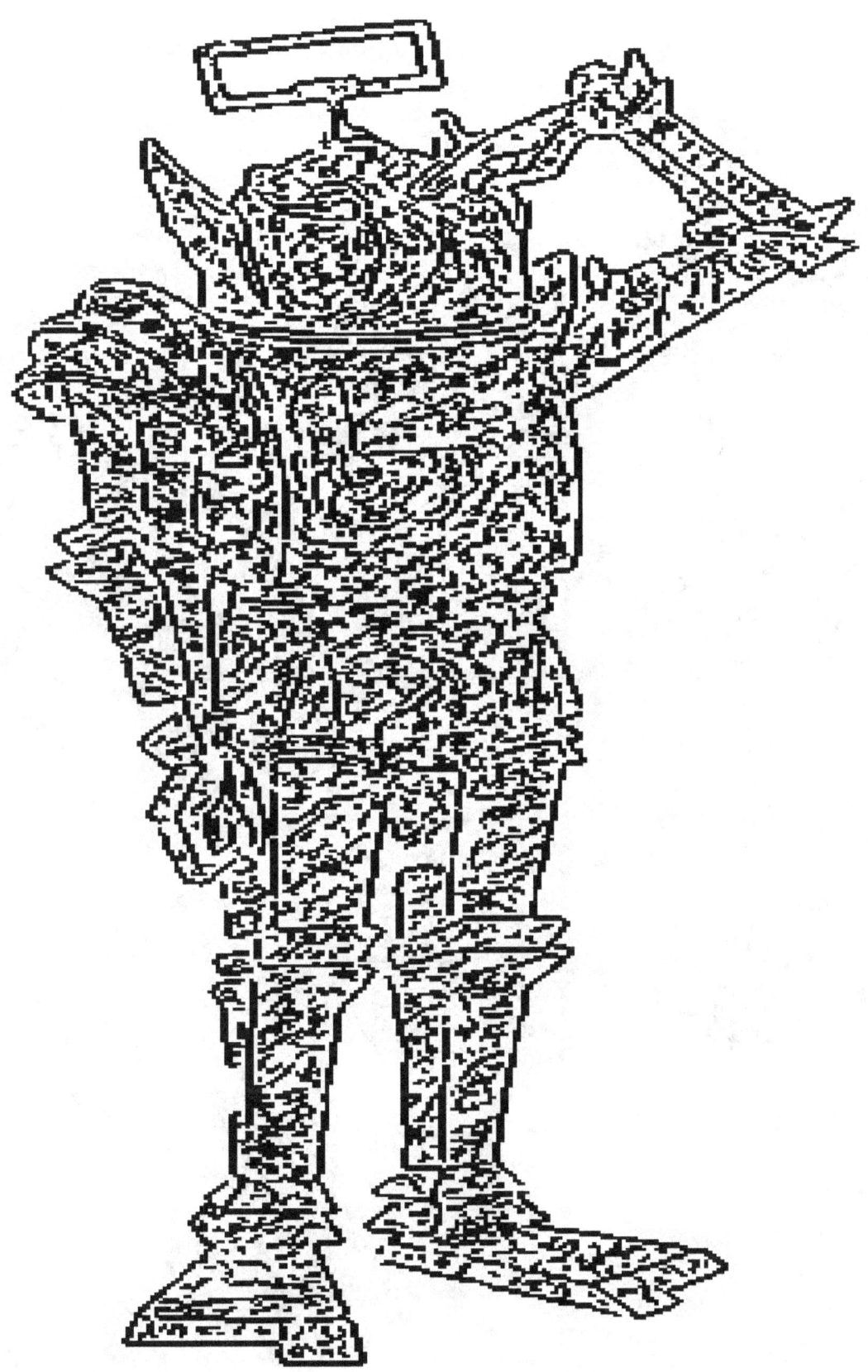

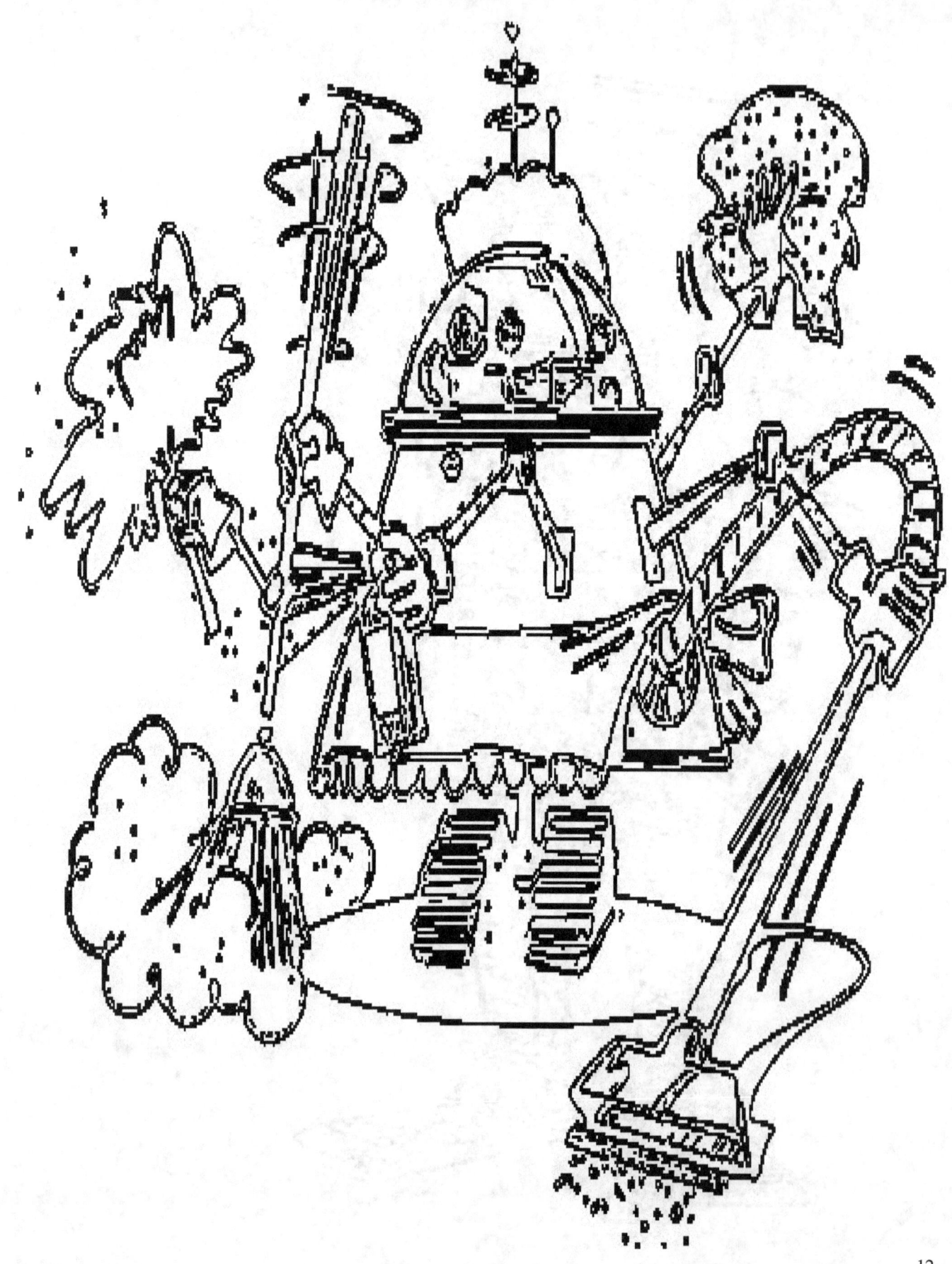

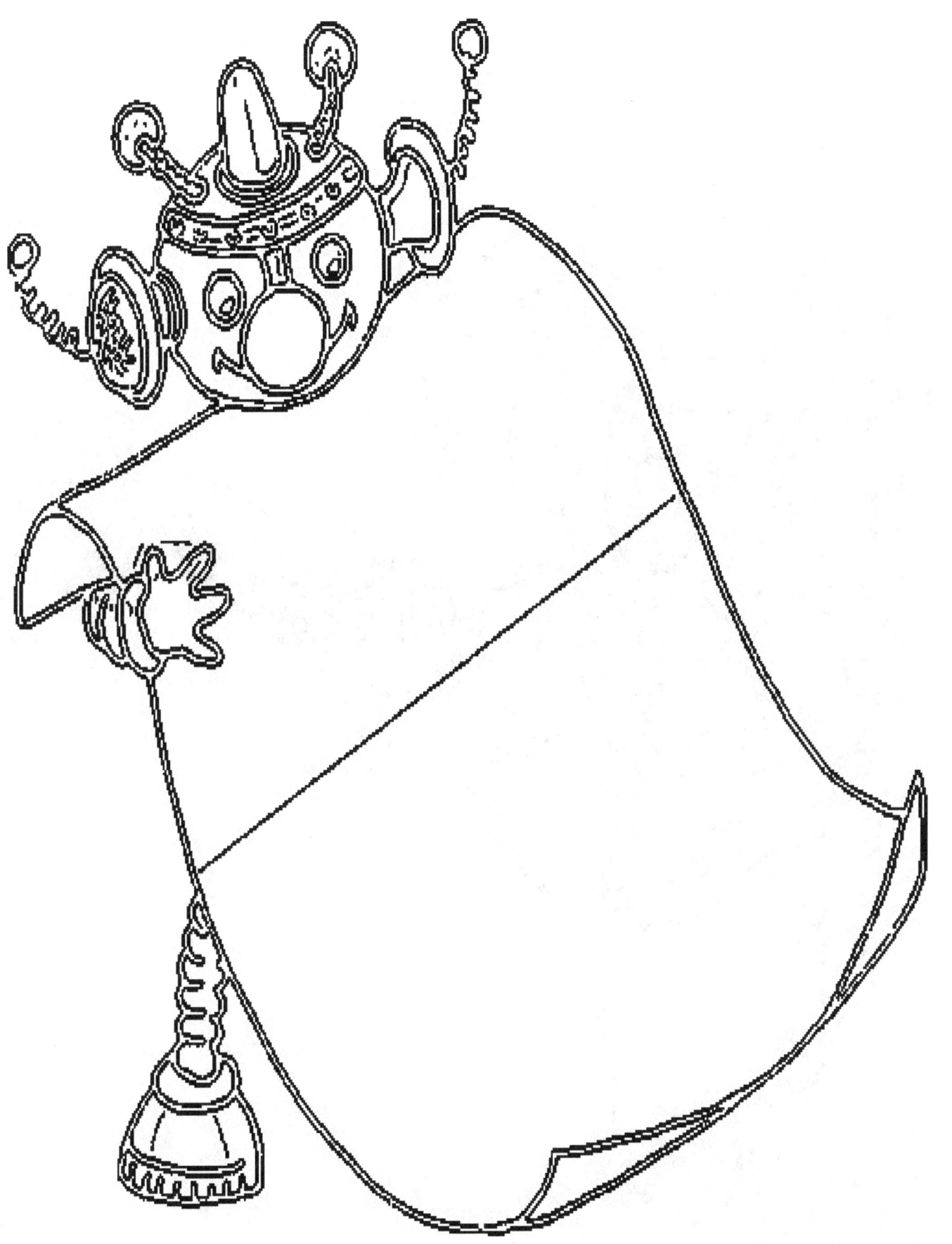

13

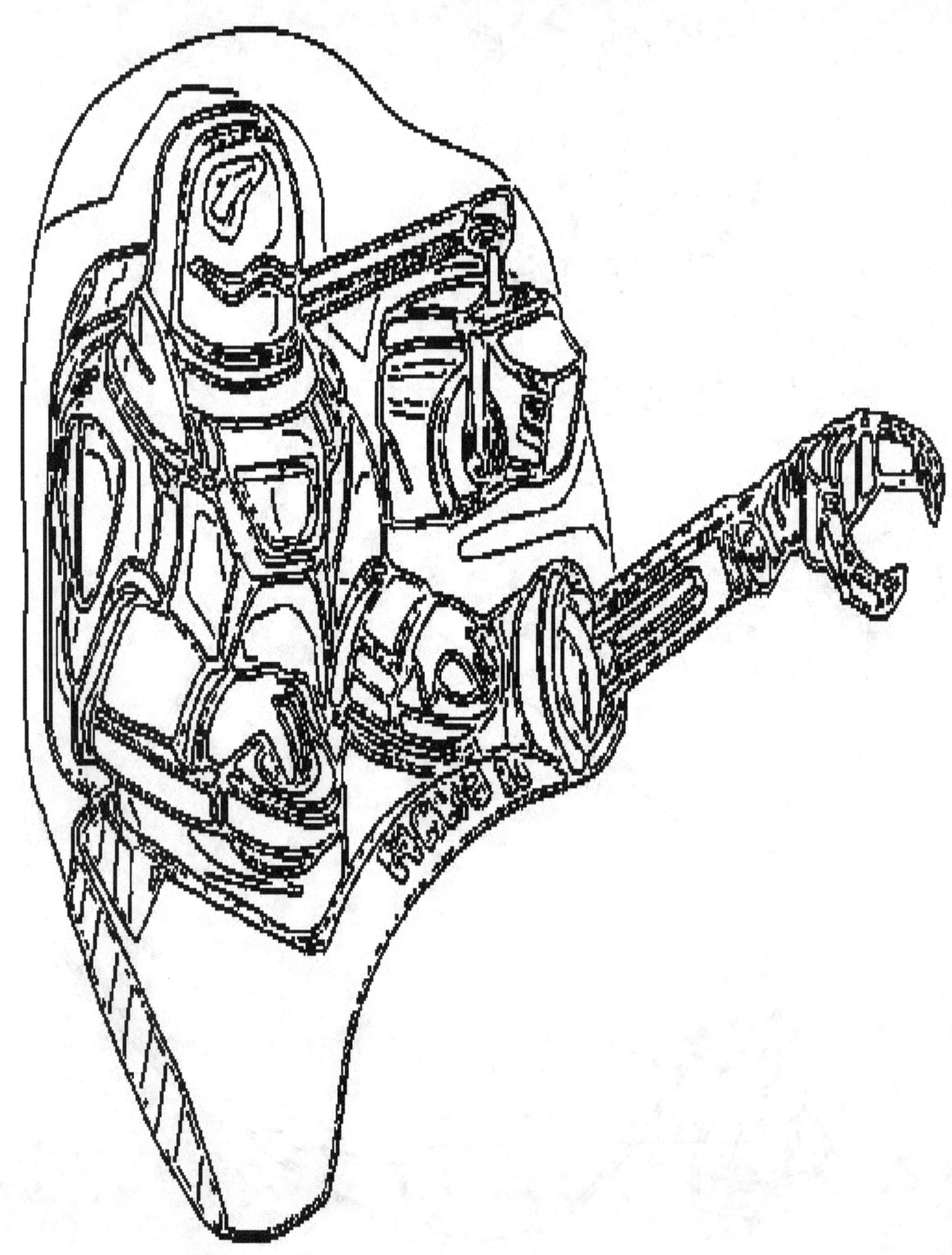

14

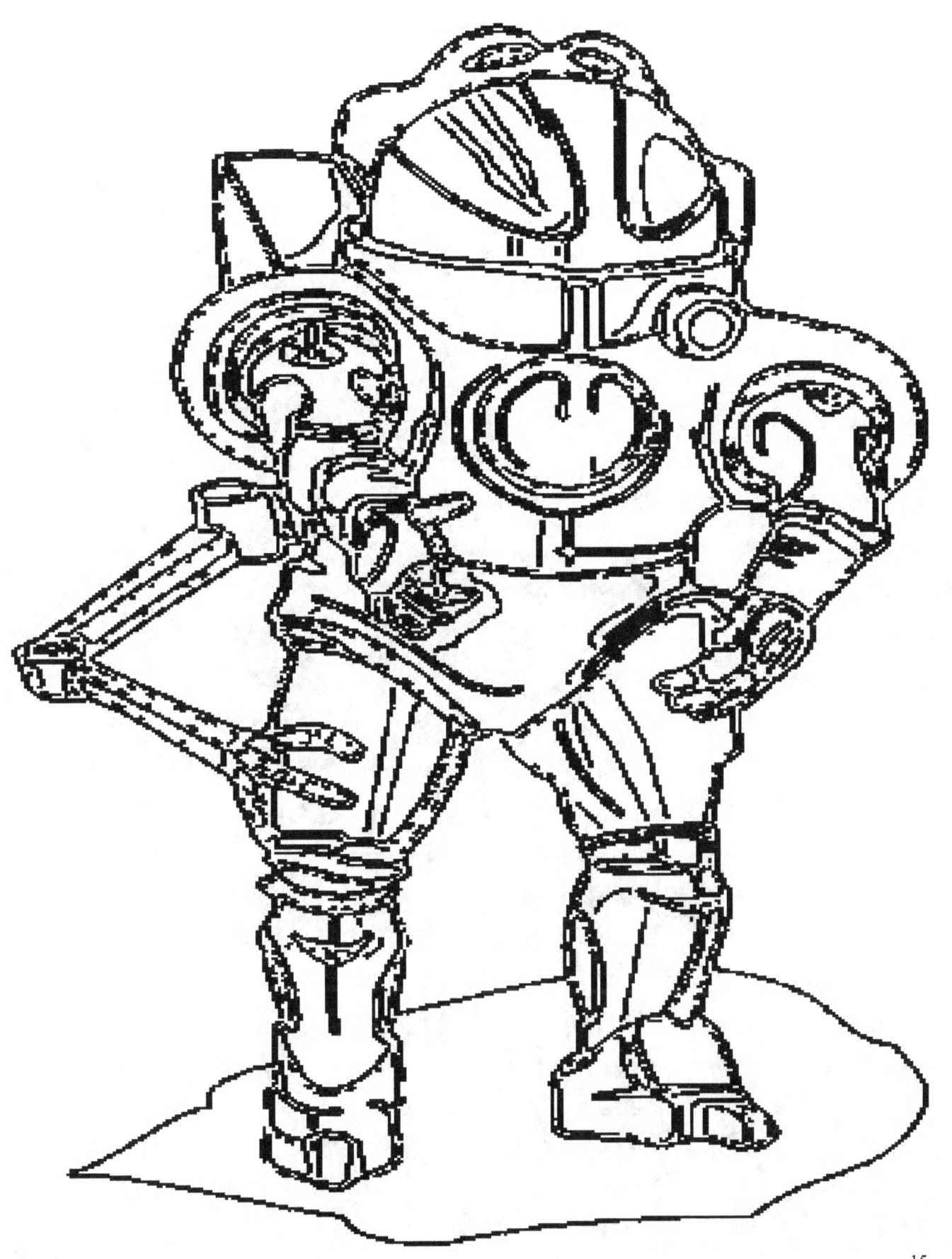

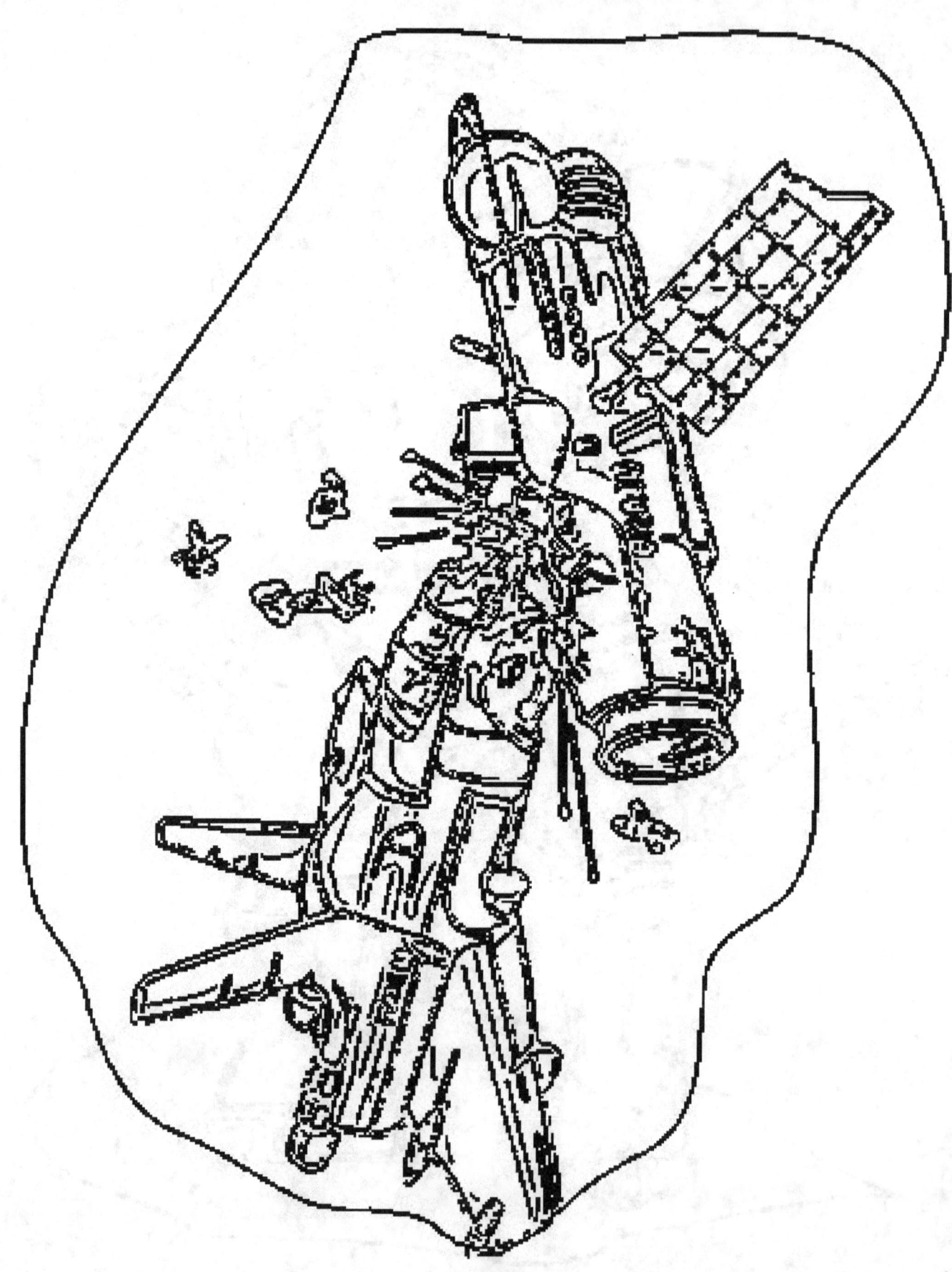

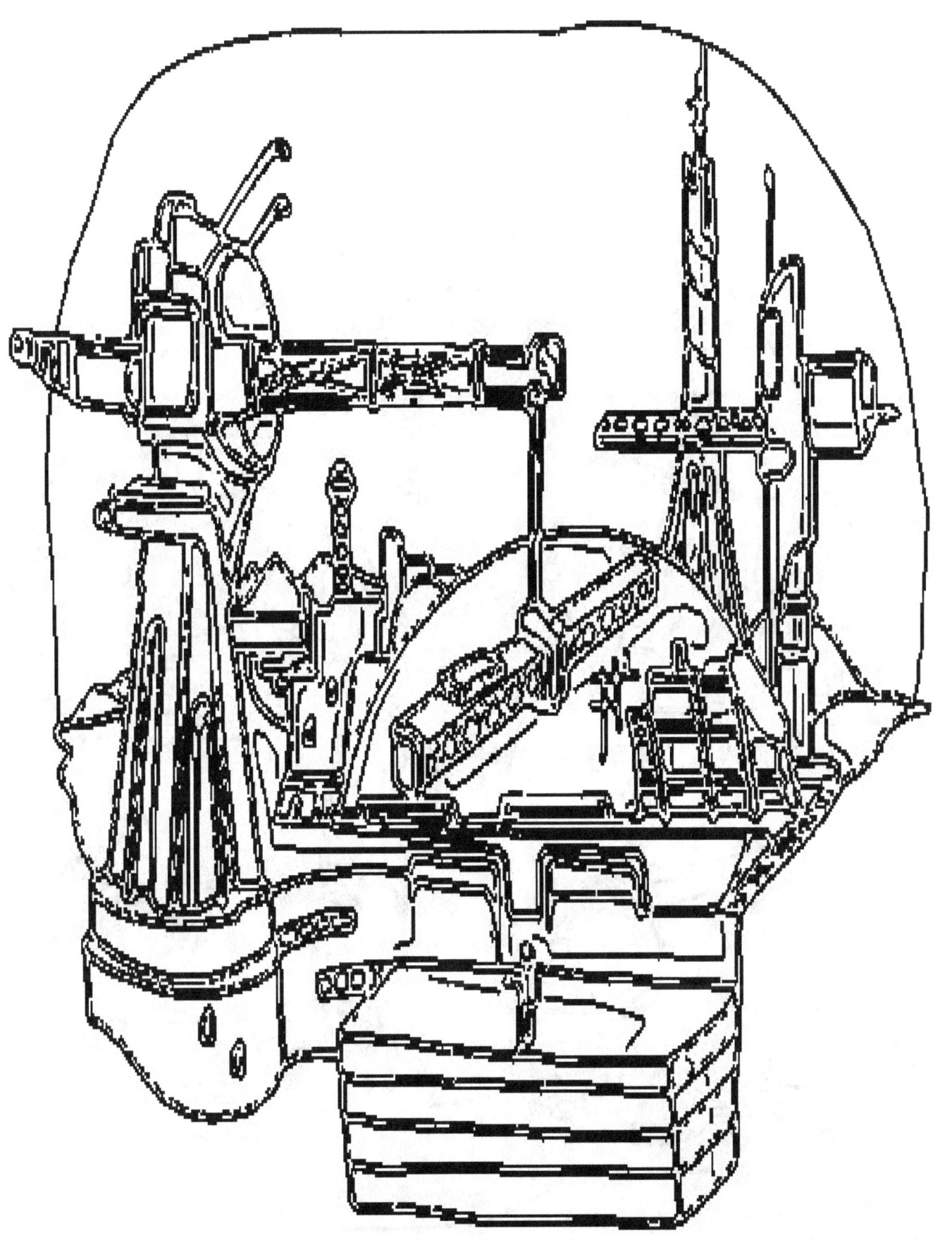

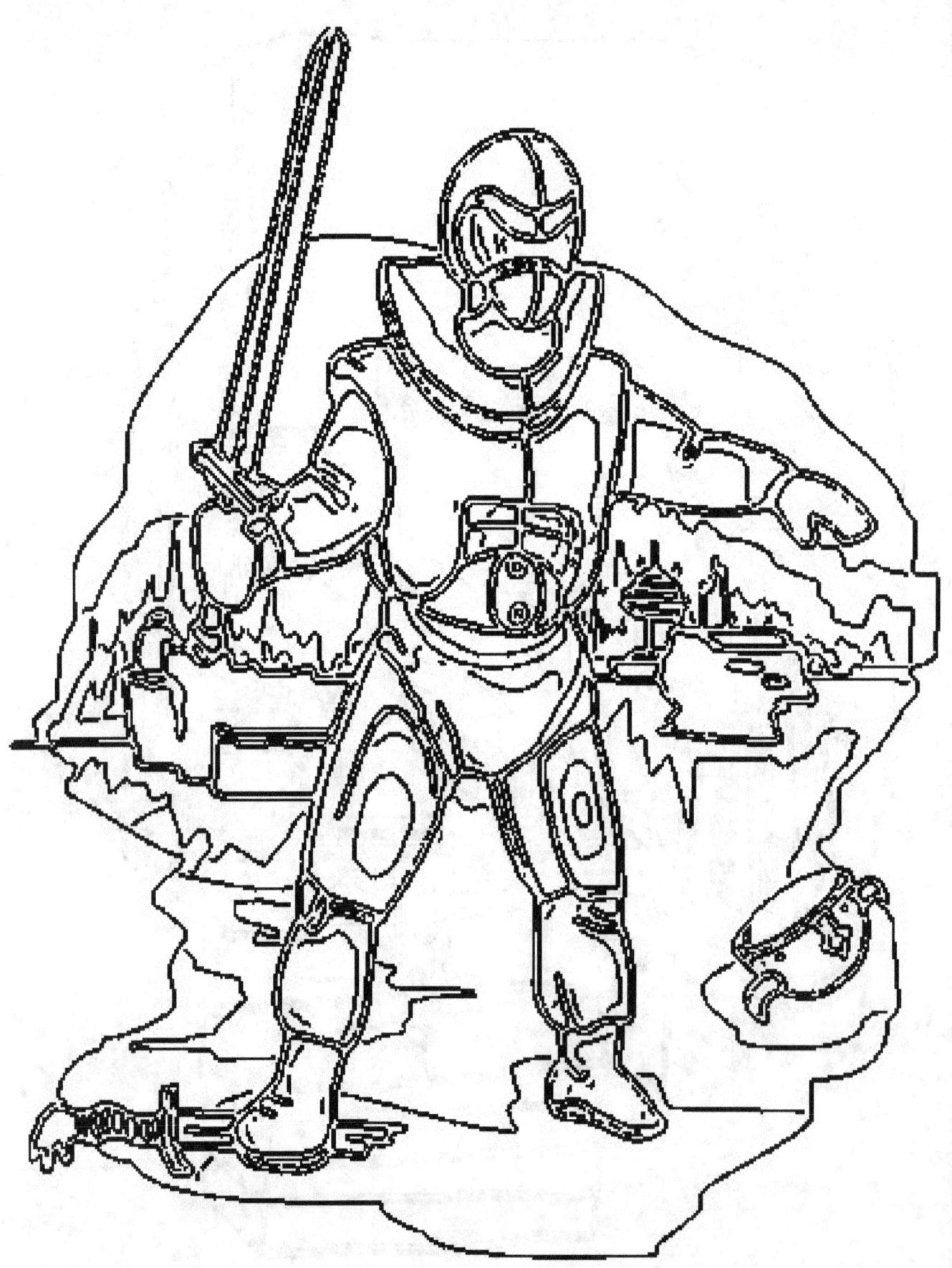

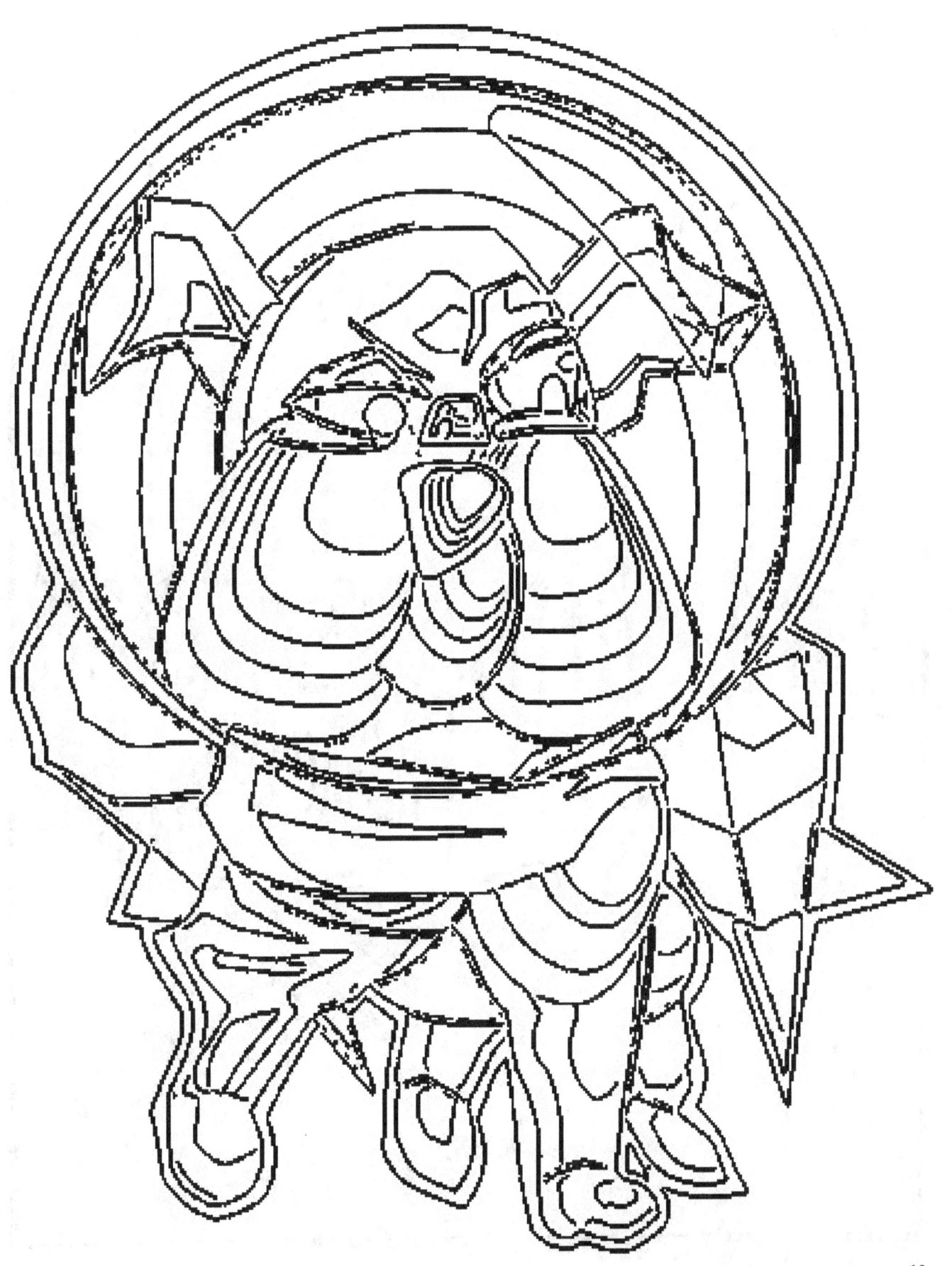

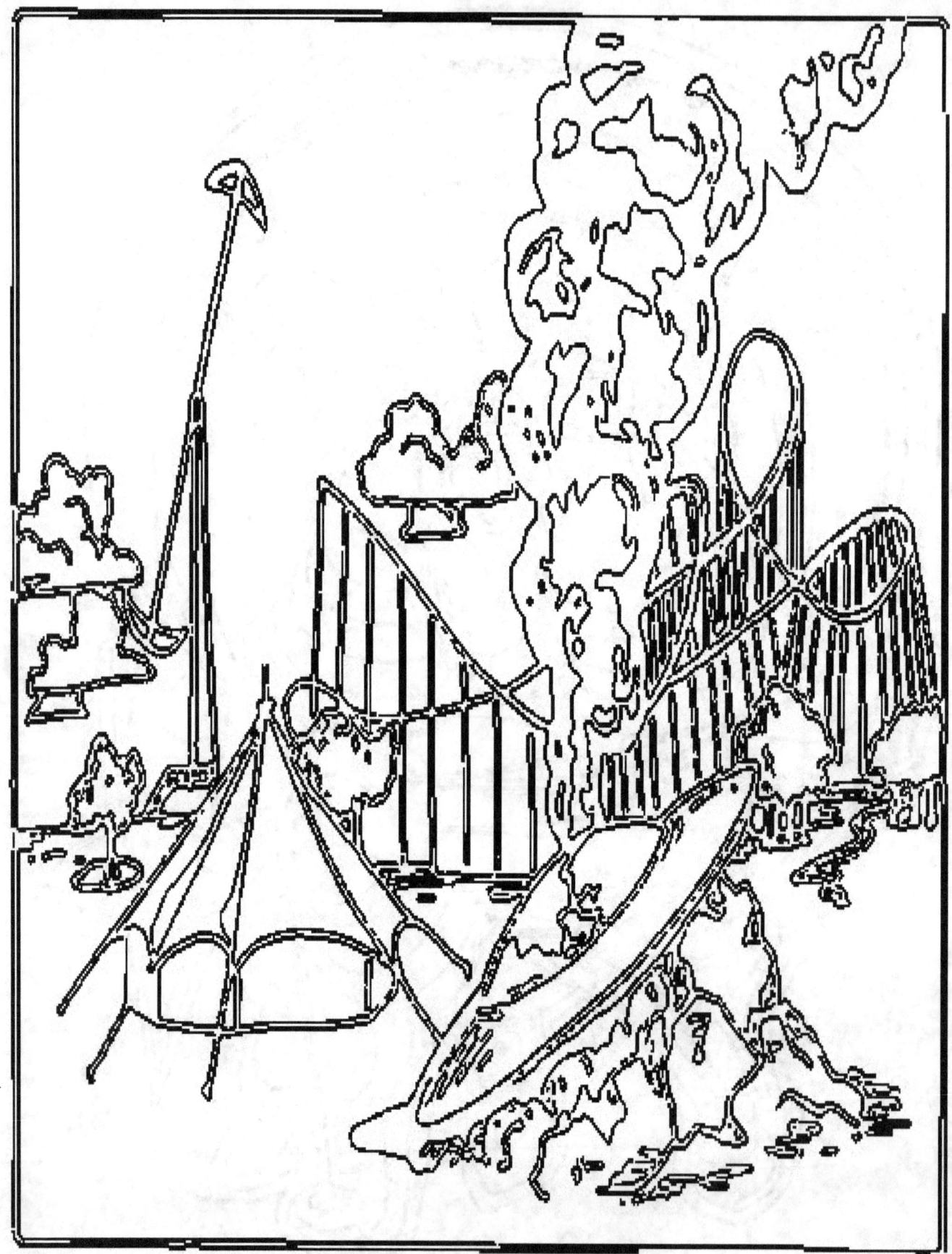

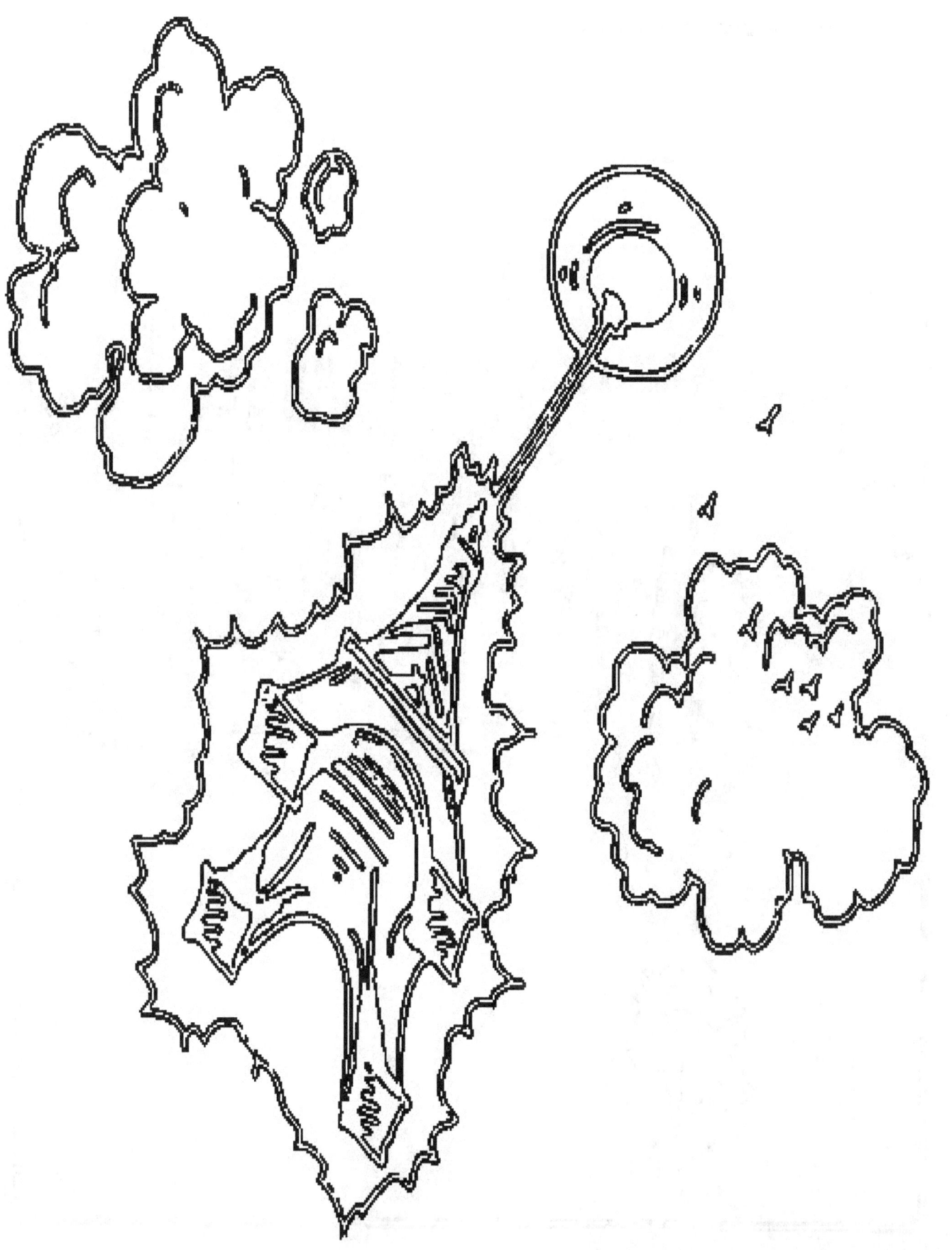

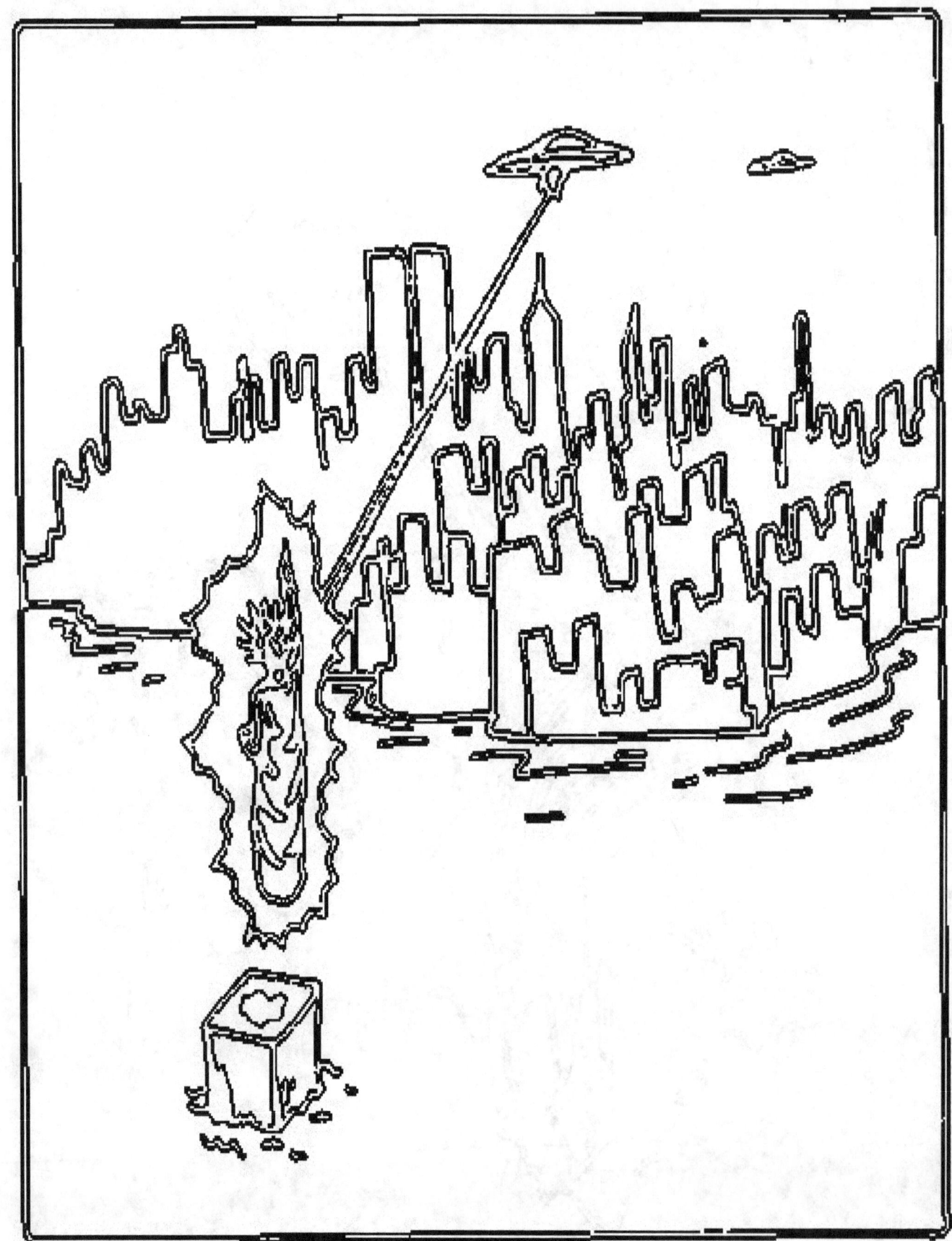

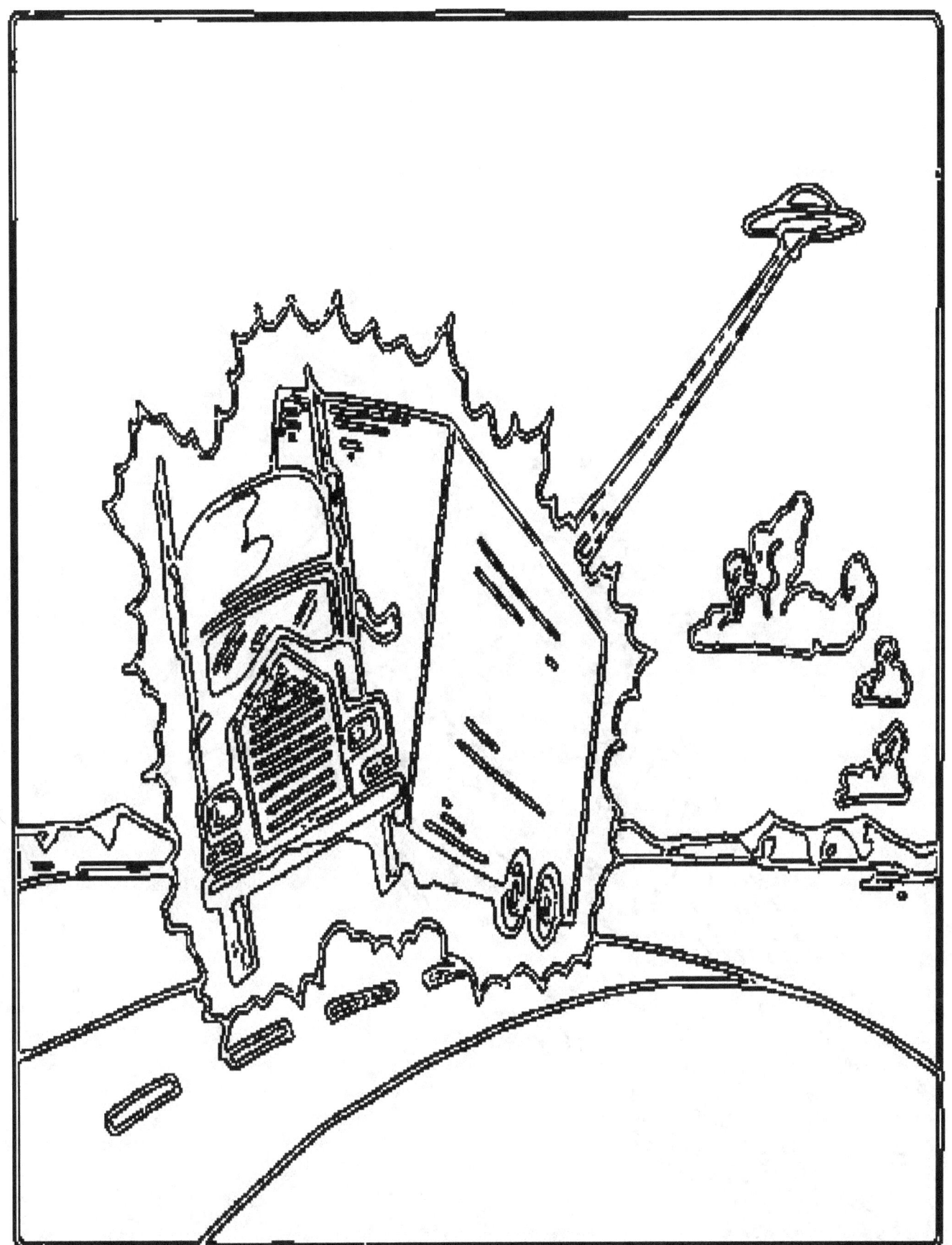

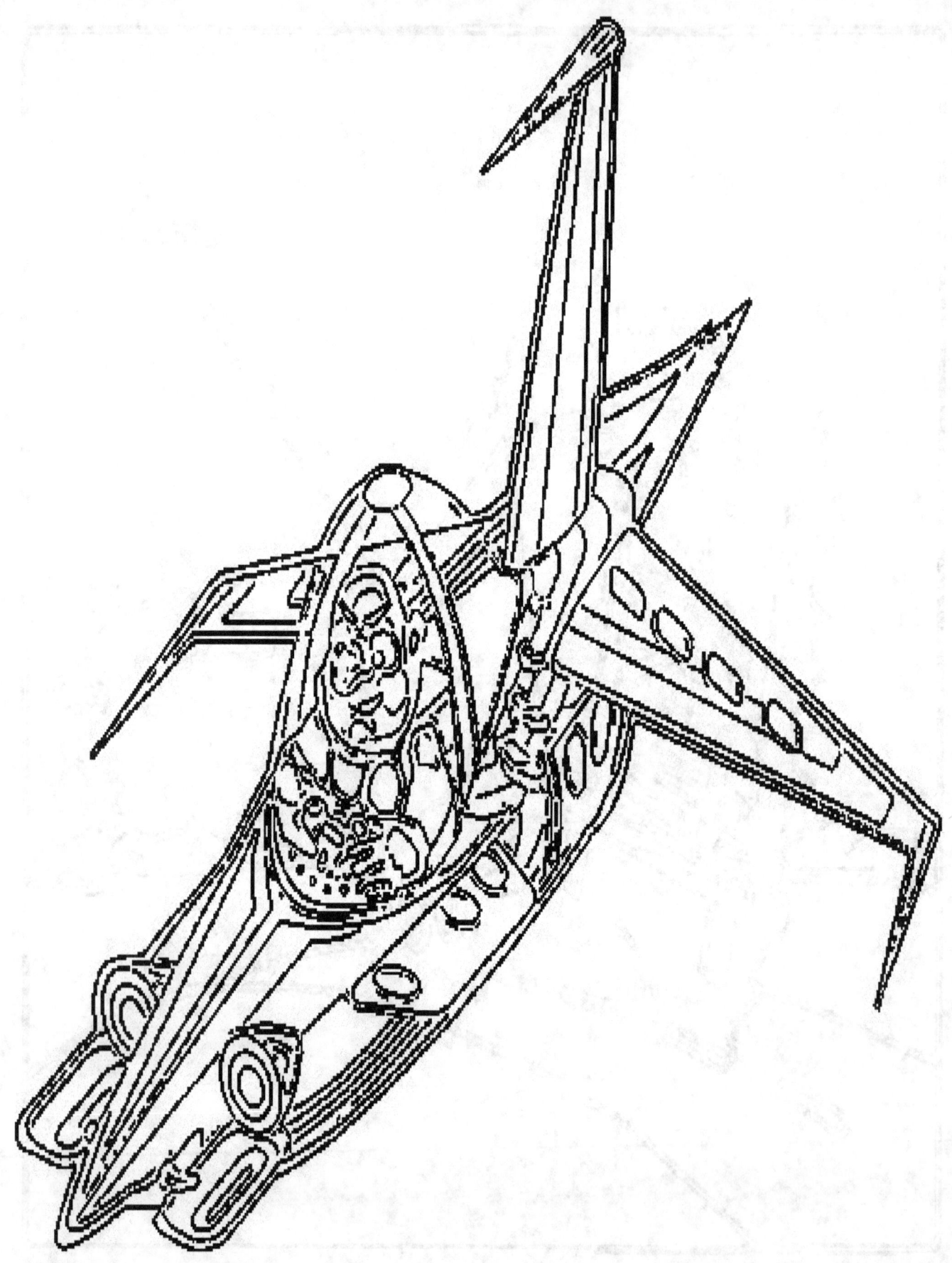

24

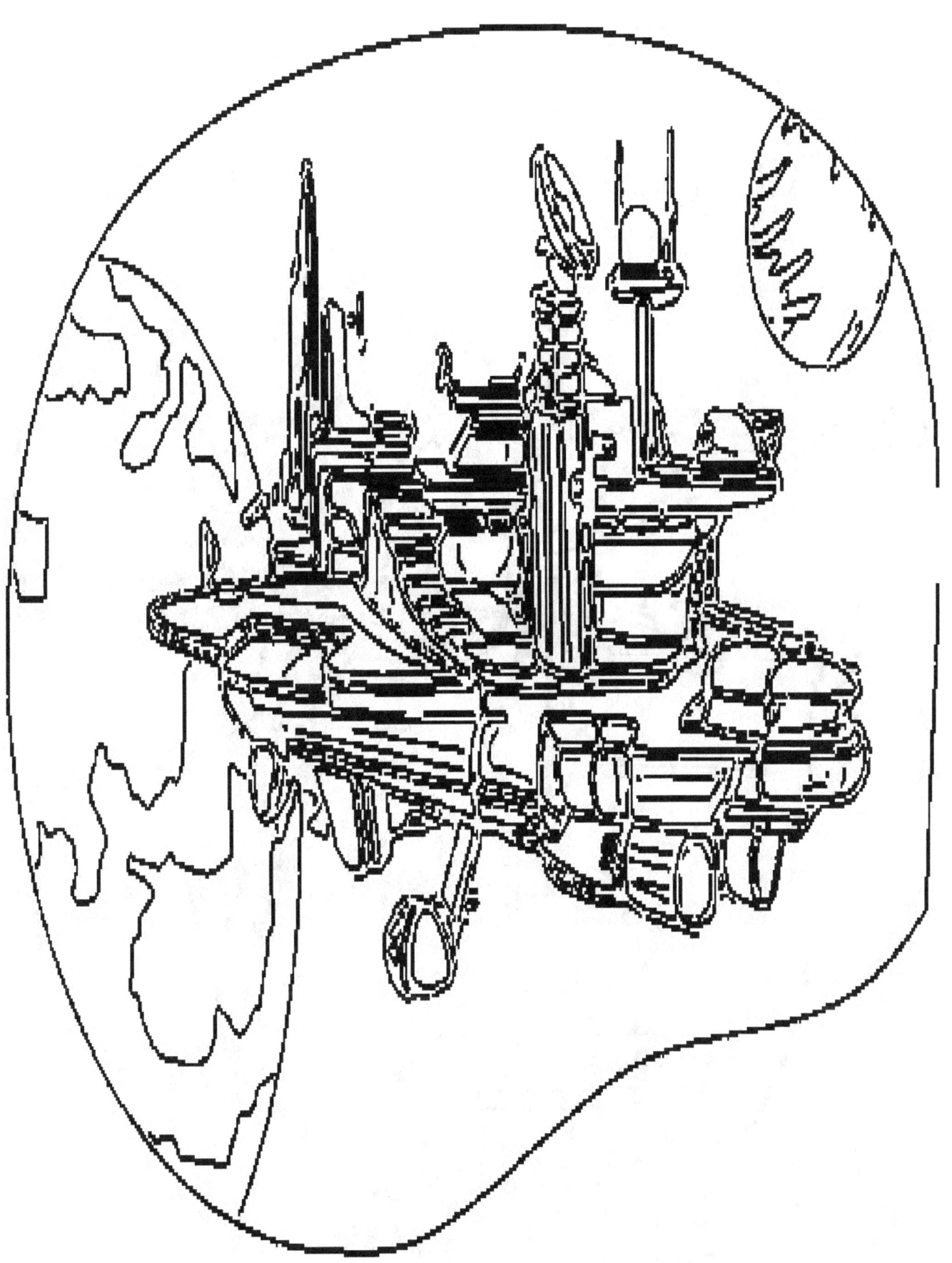

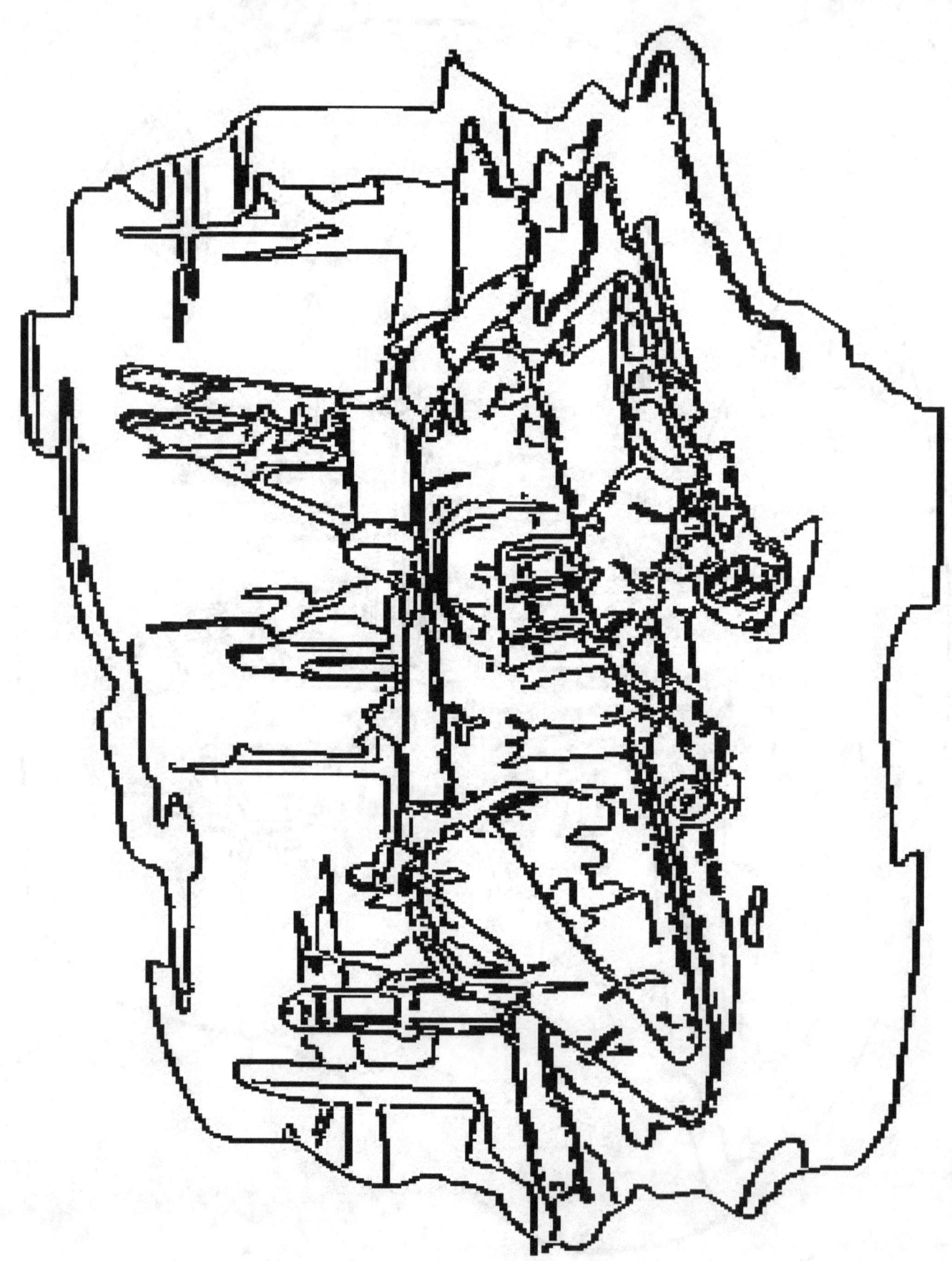

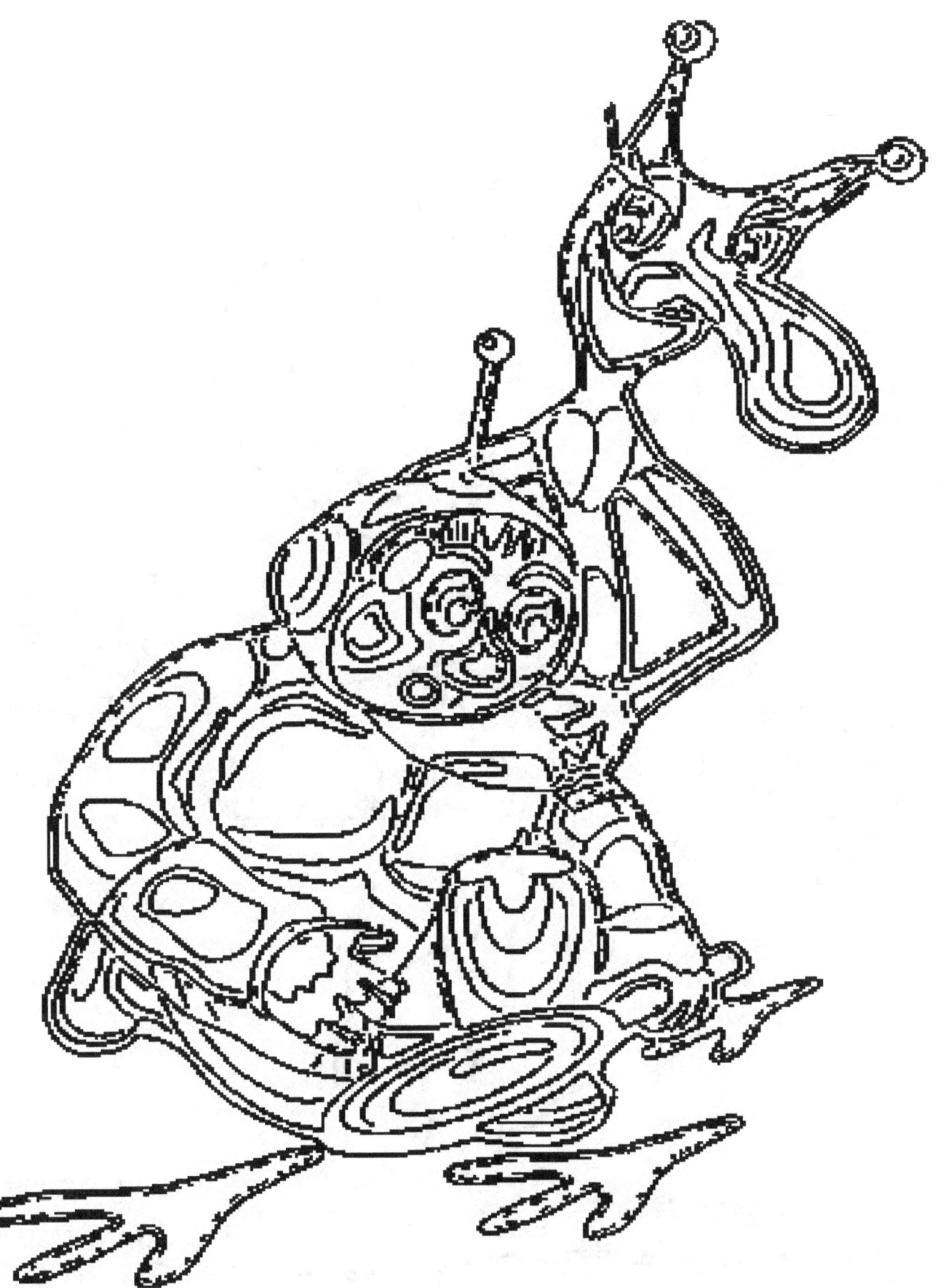

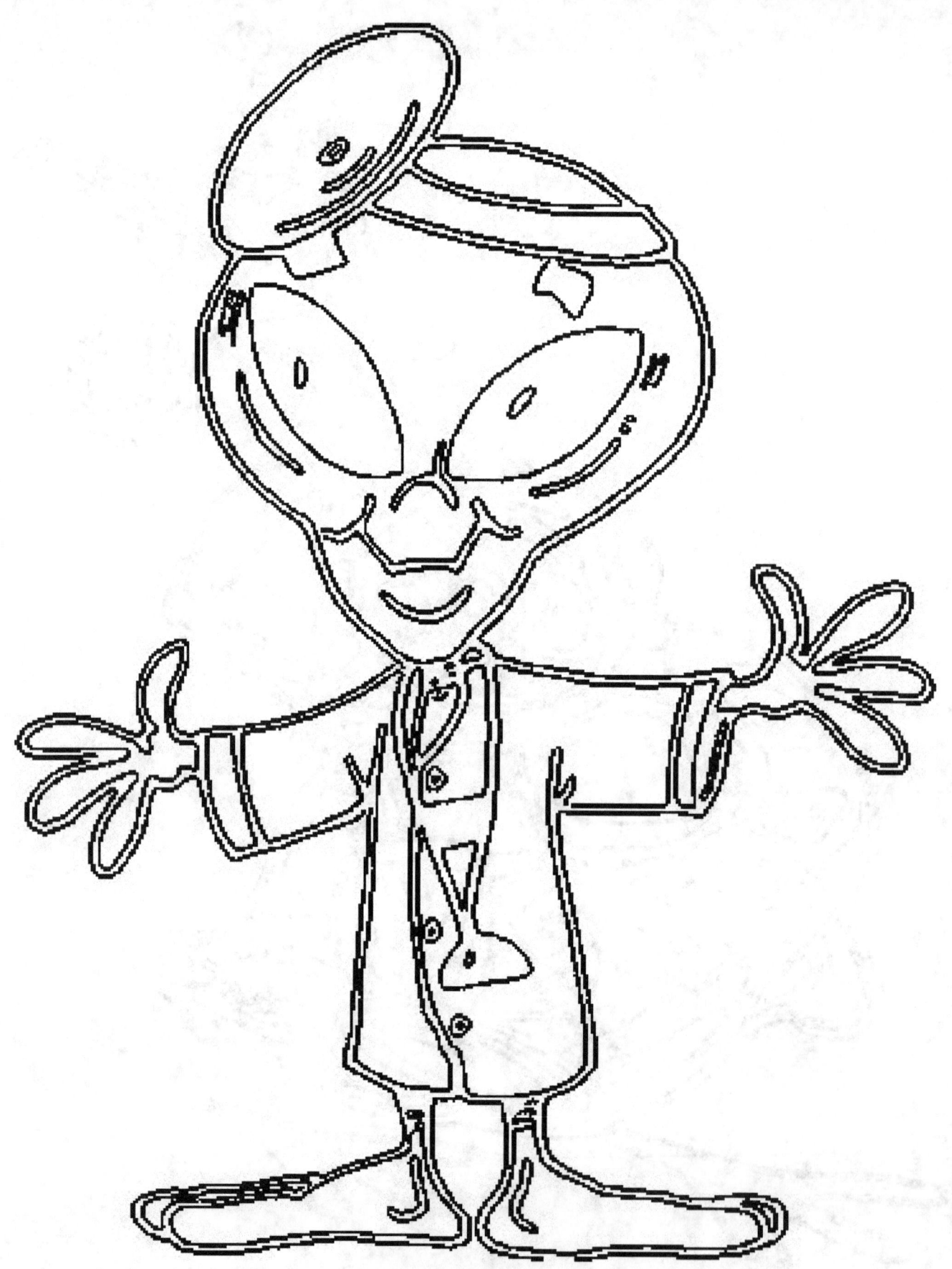

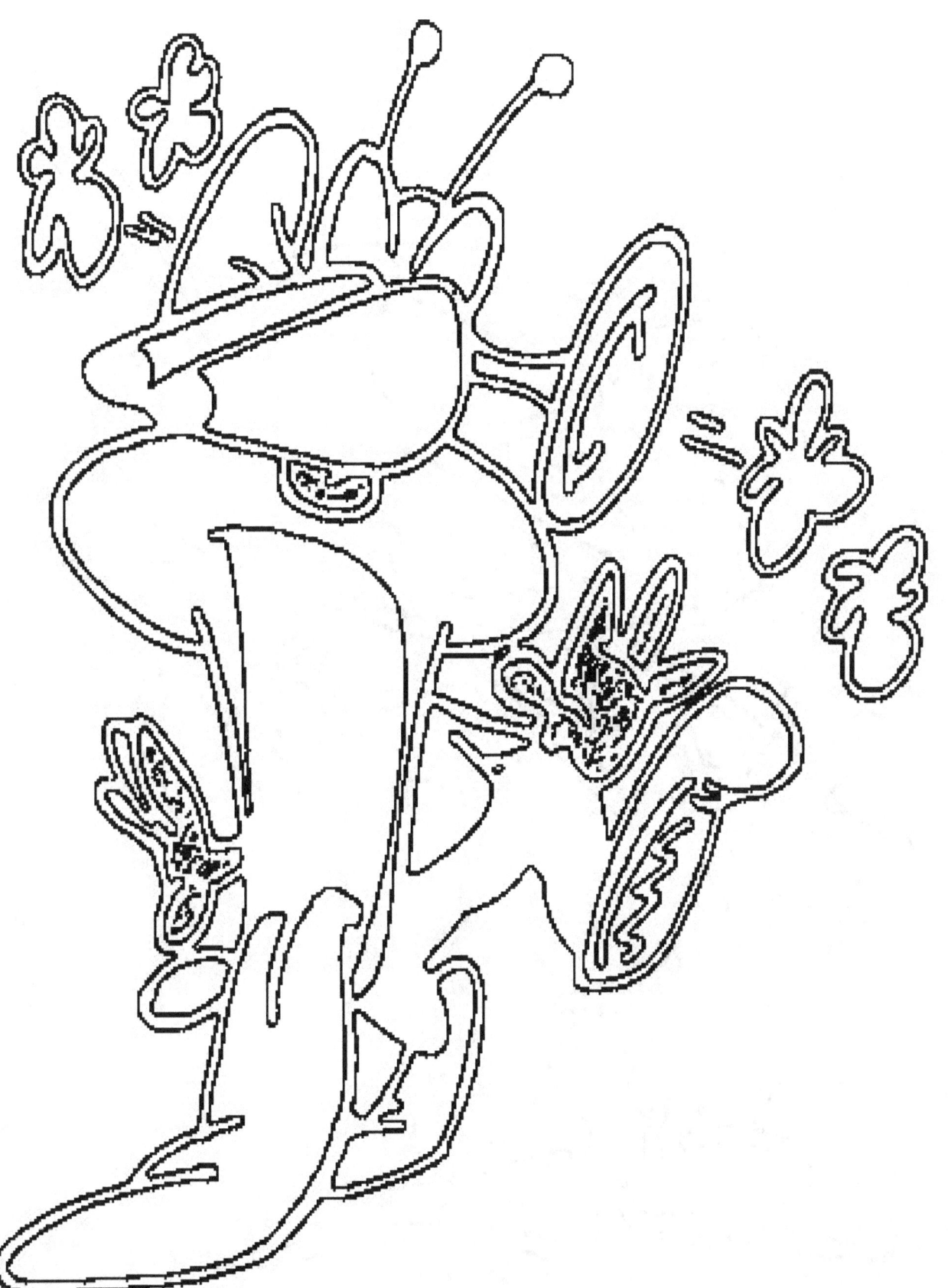

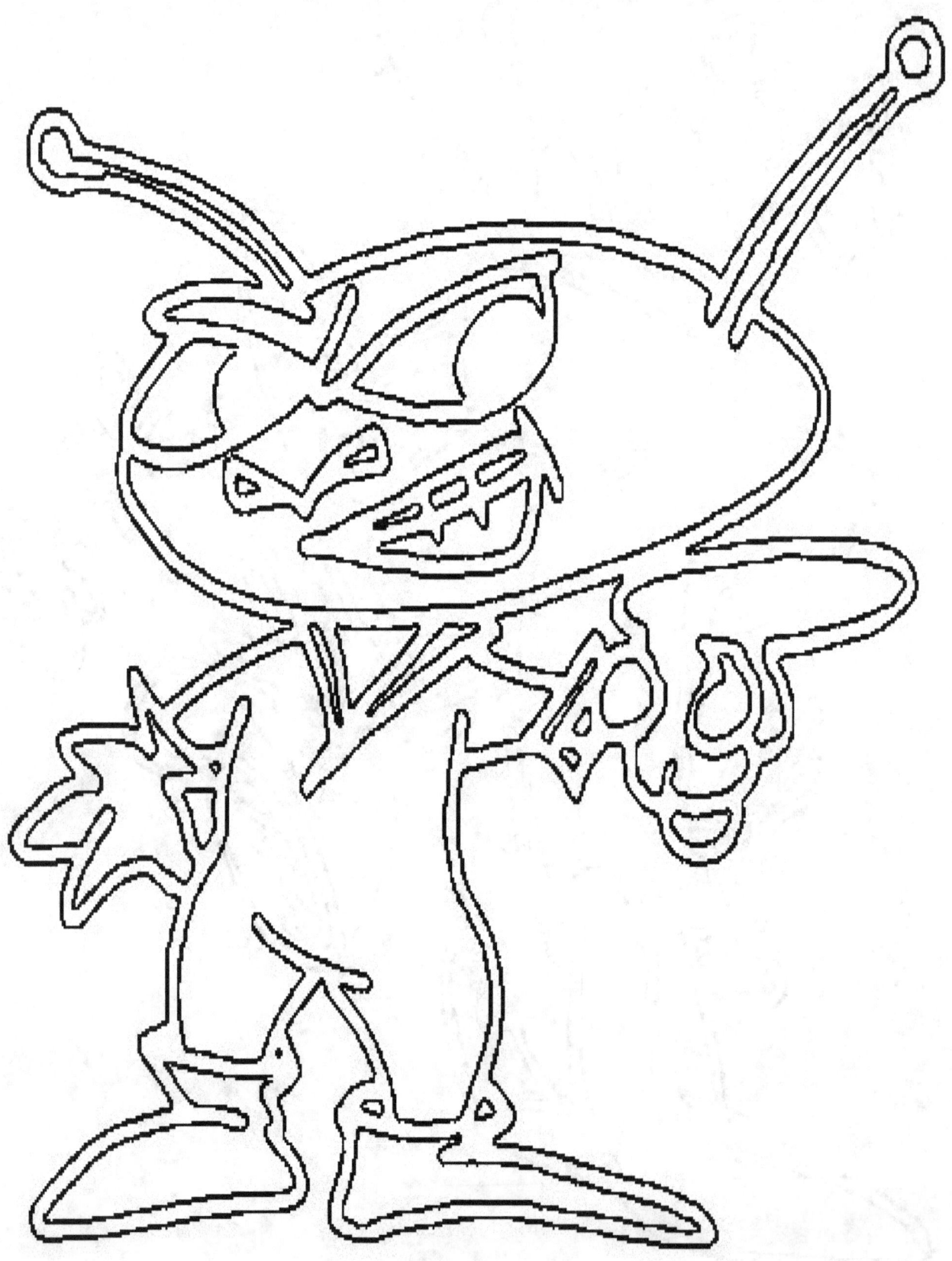

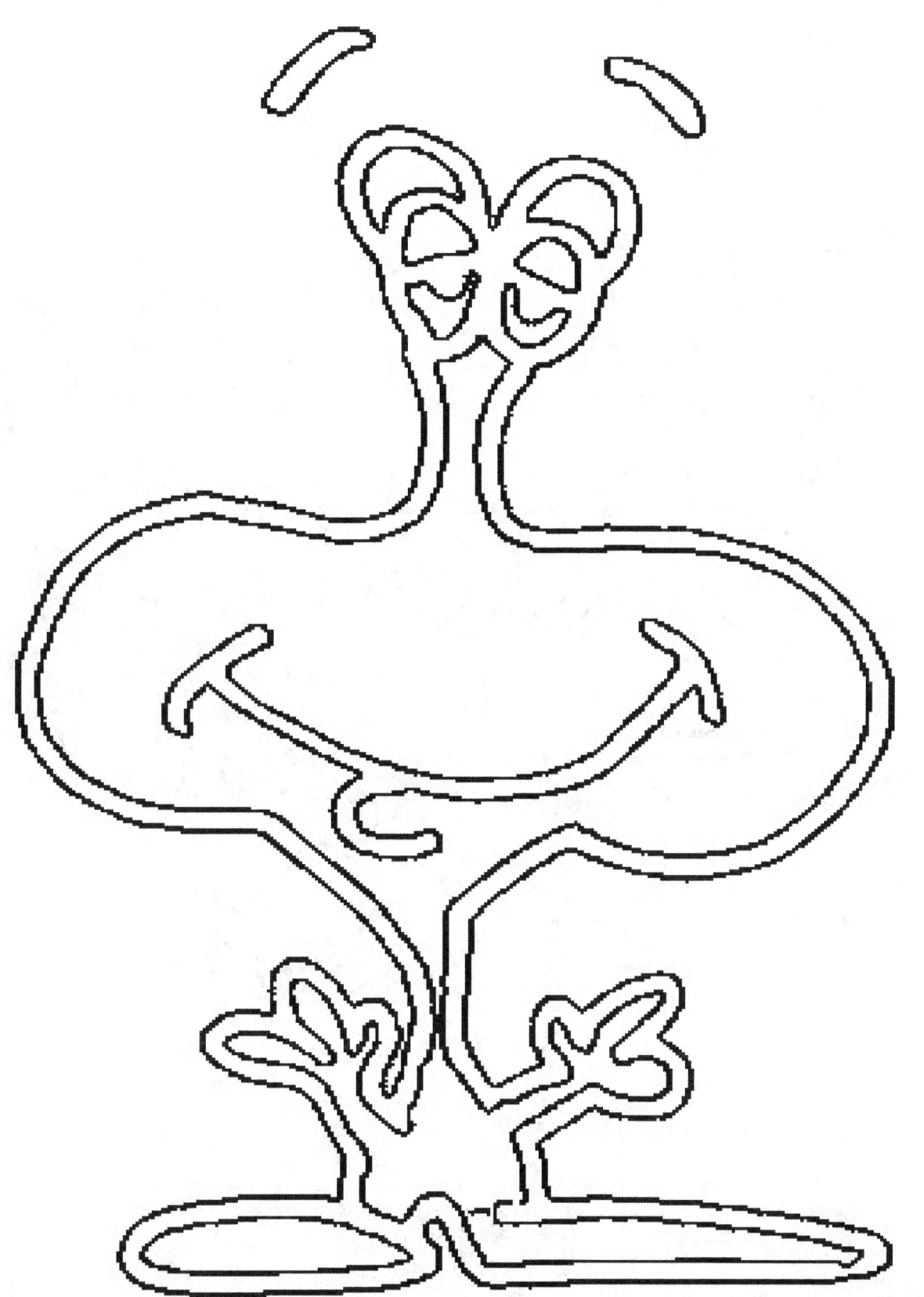

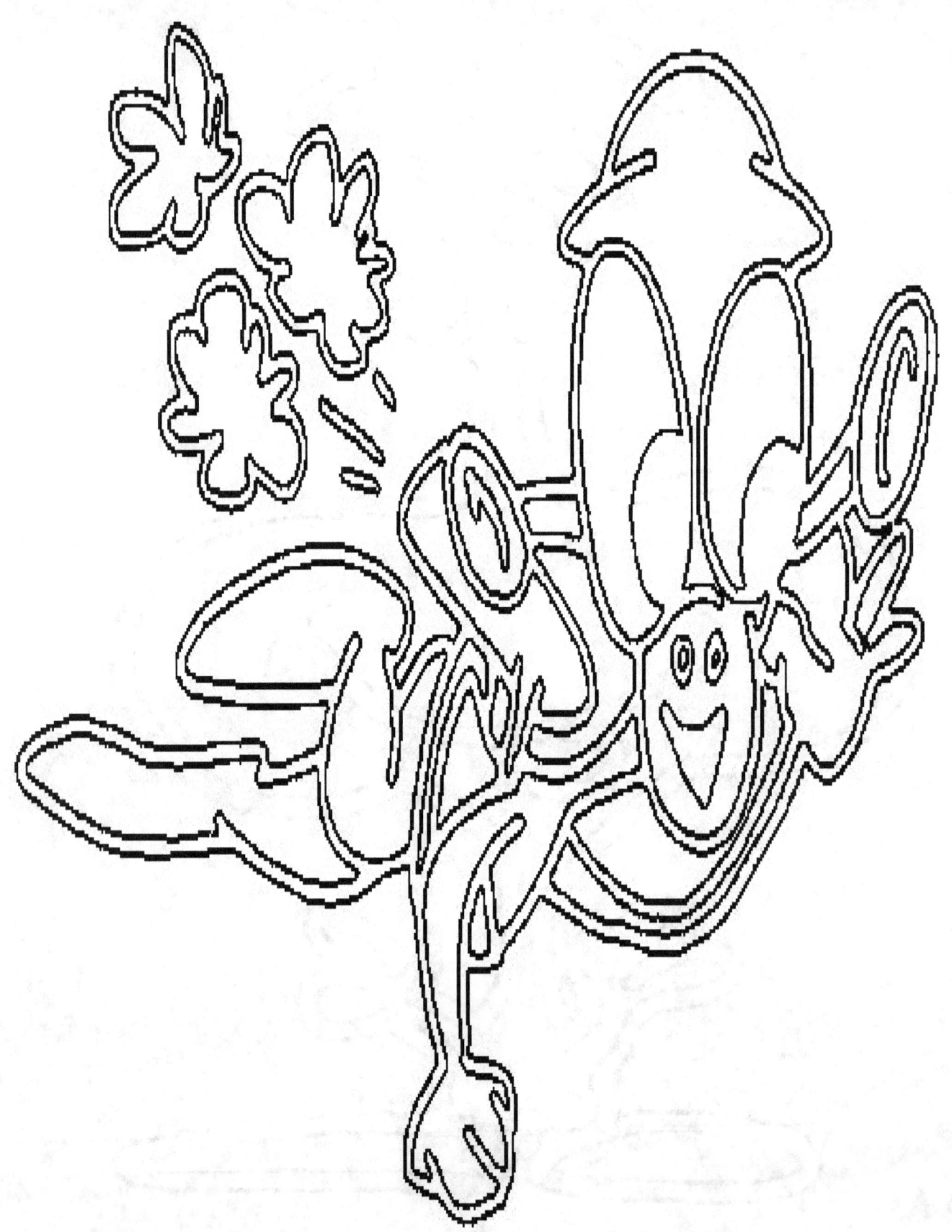

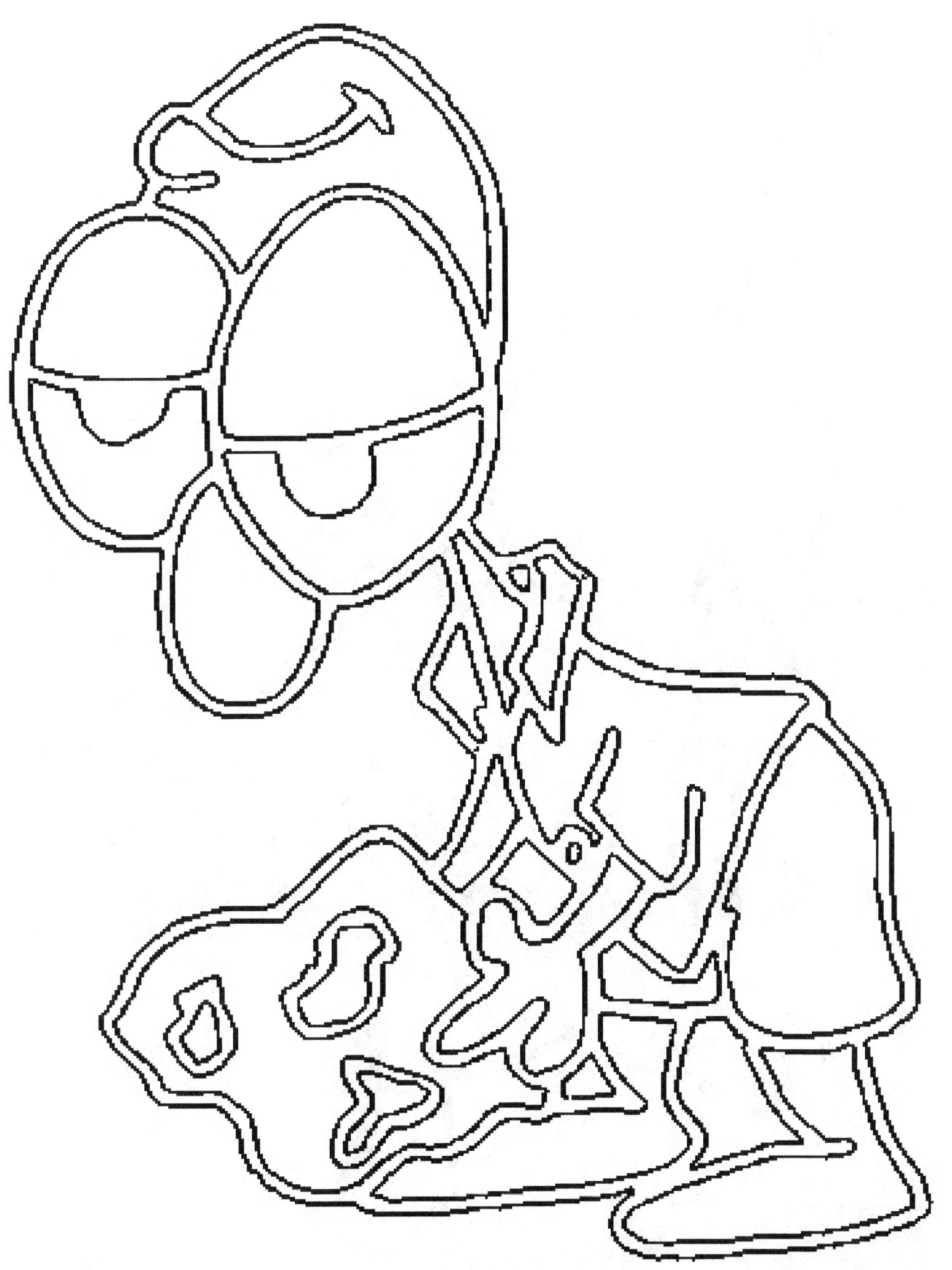

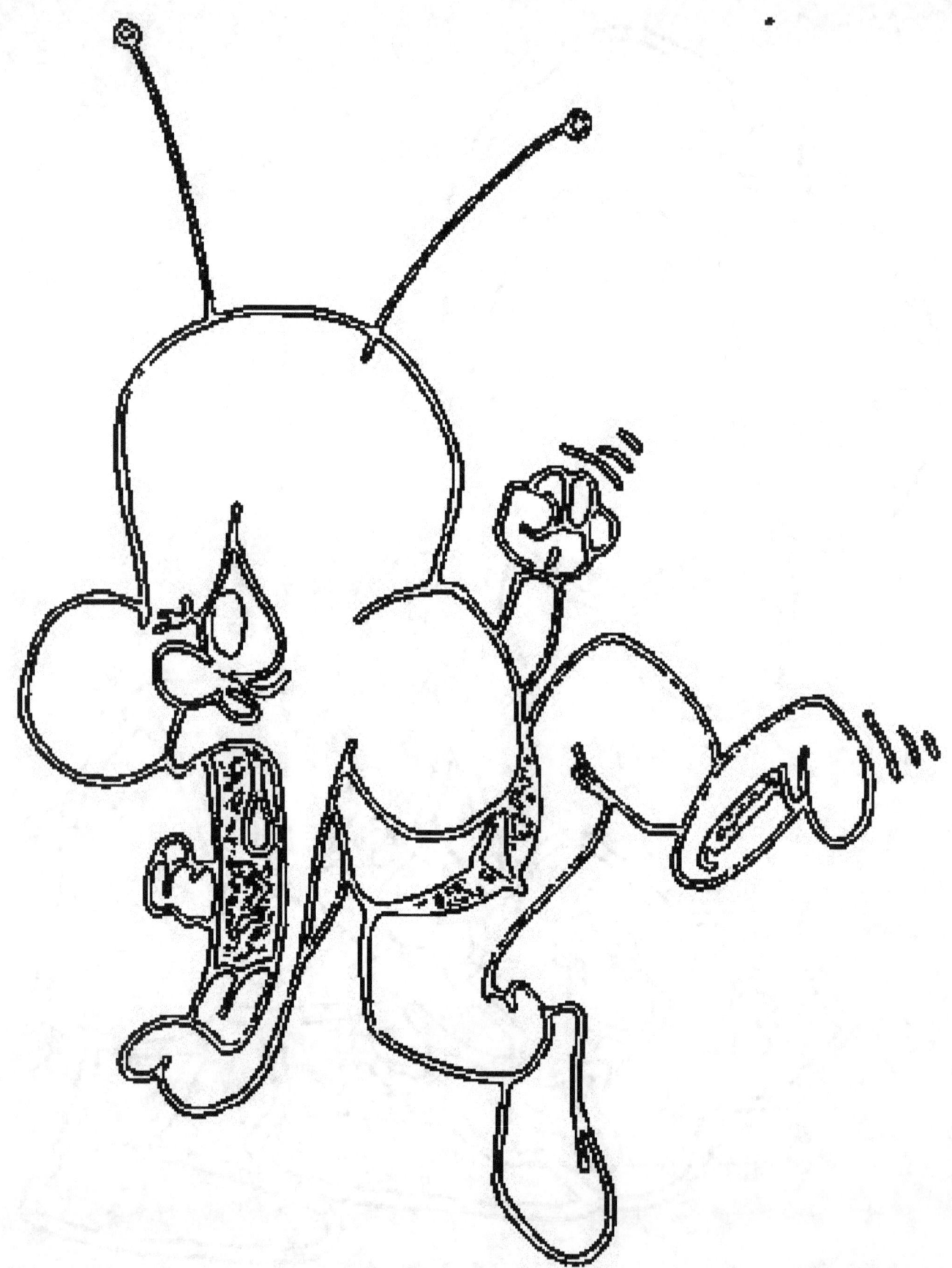

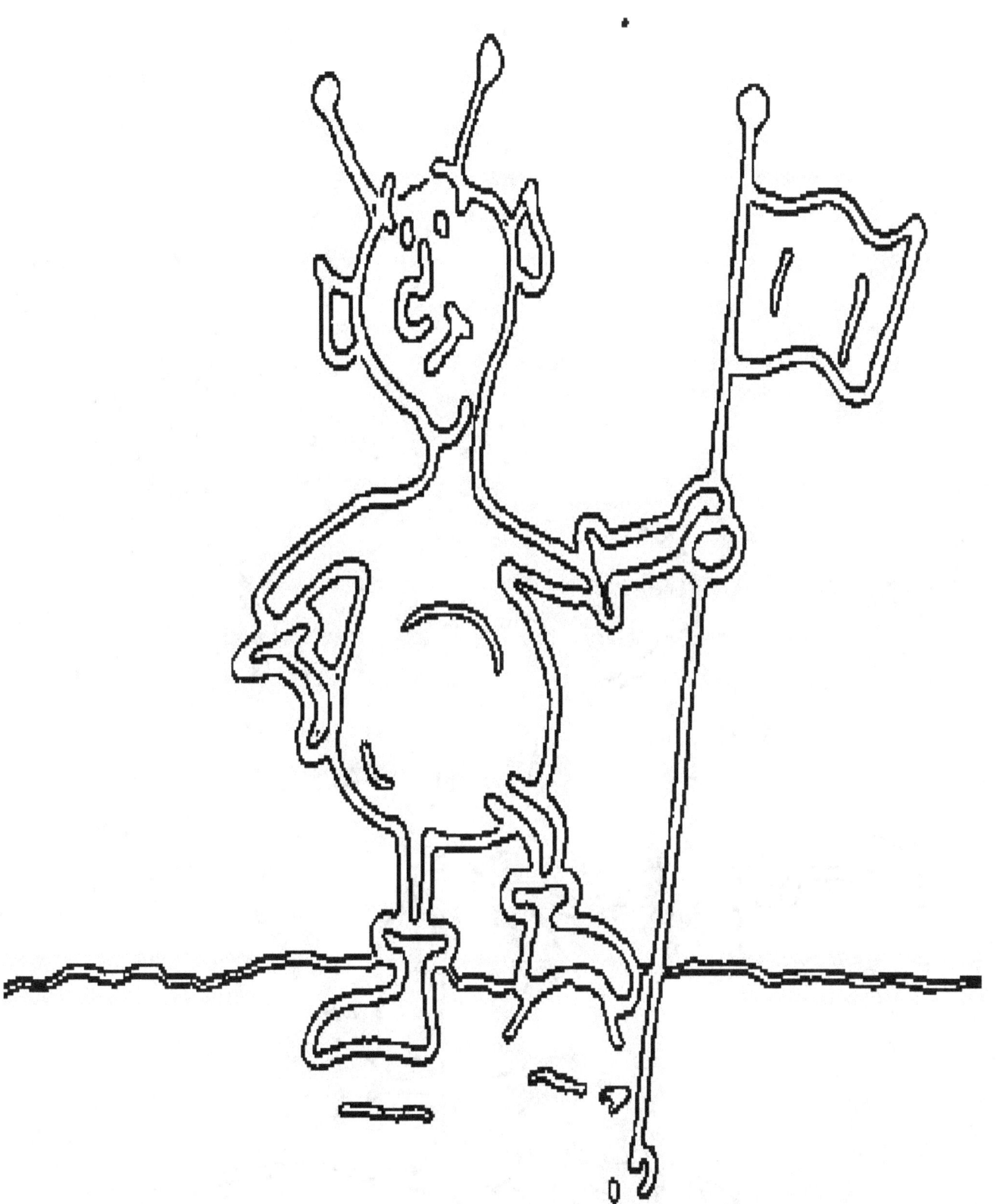

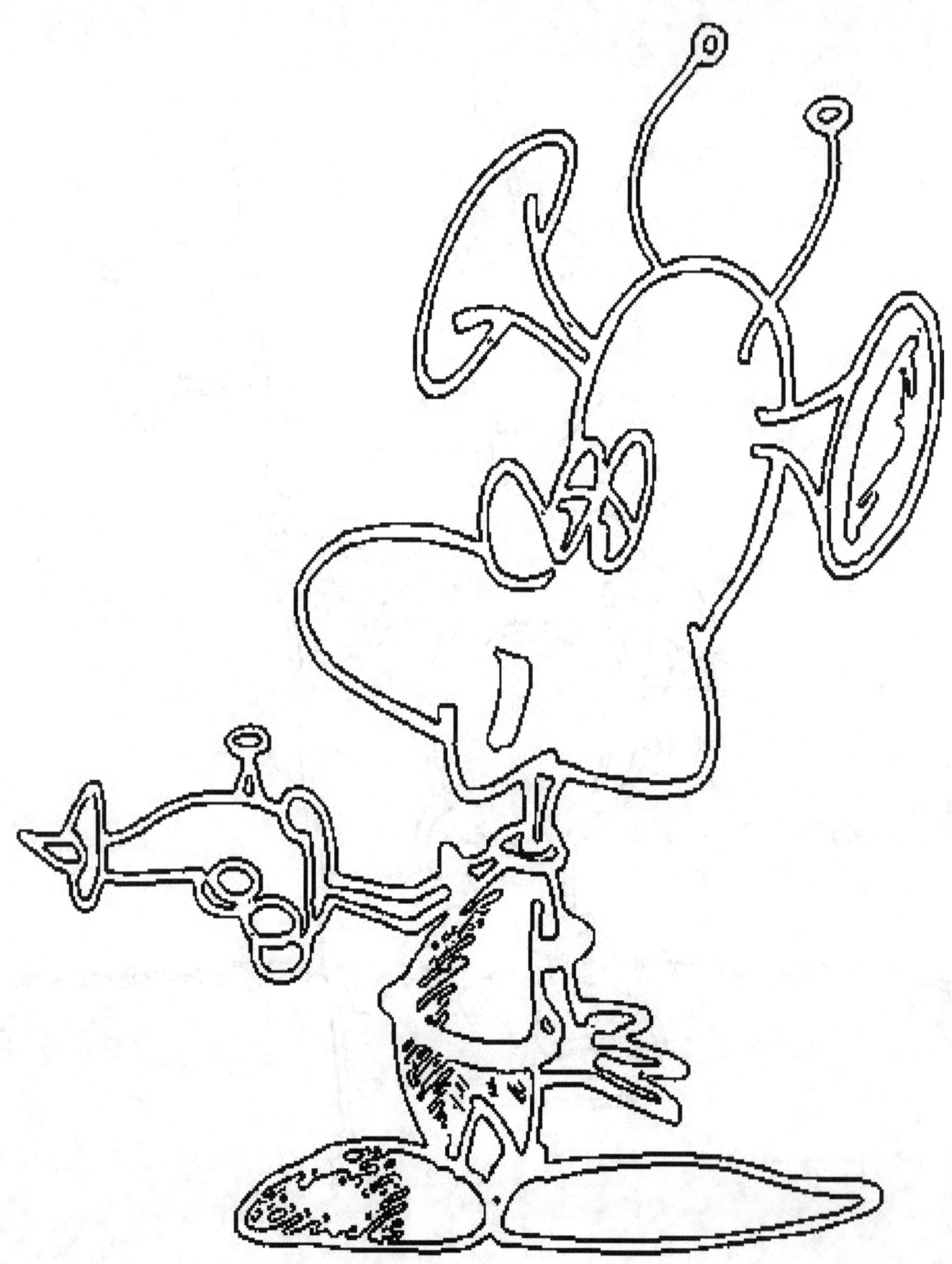

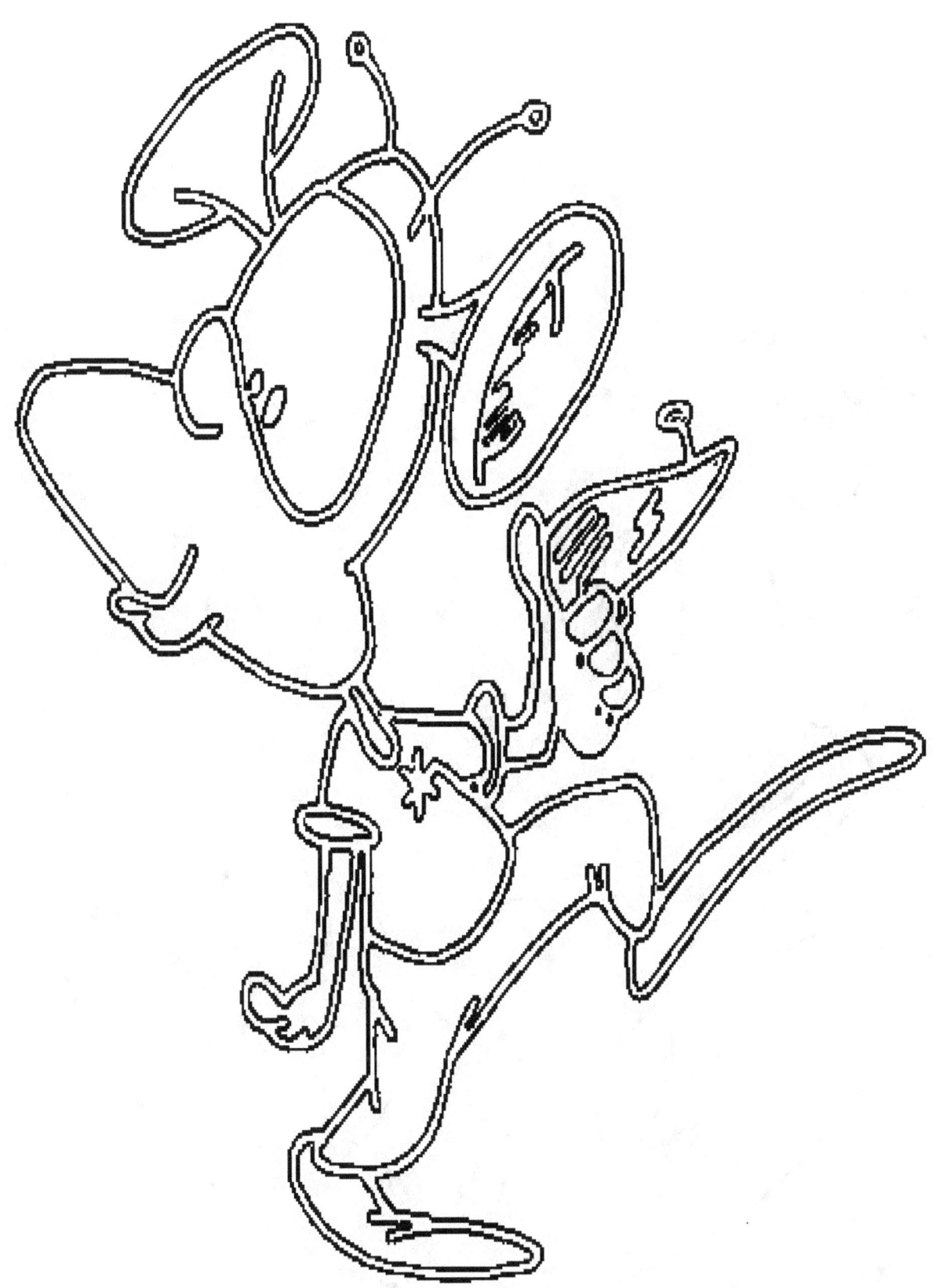

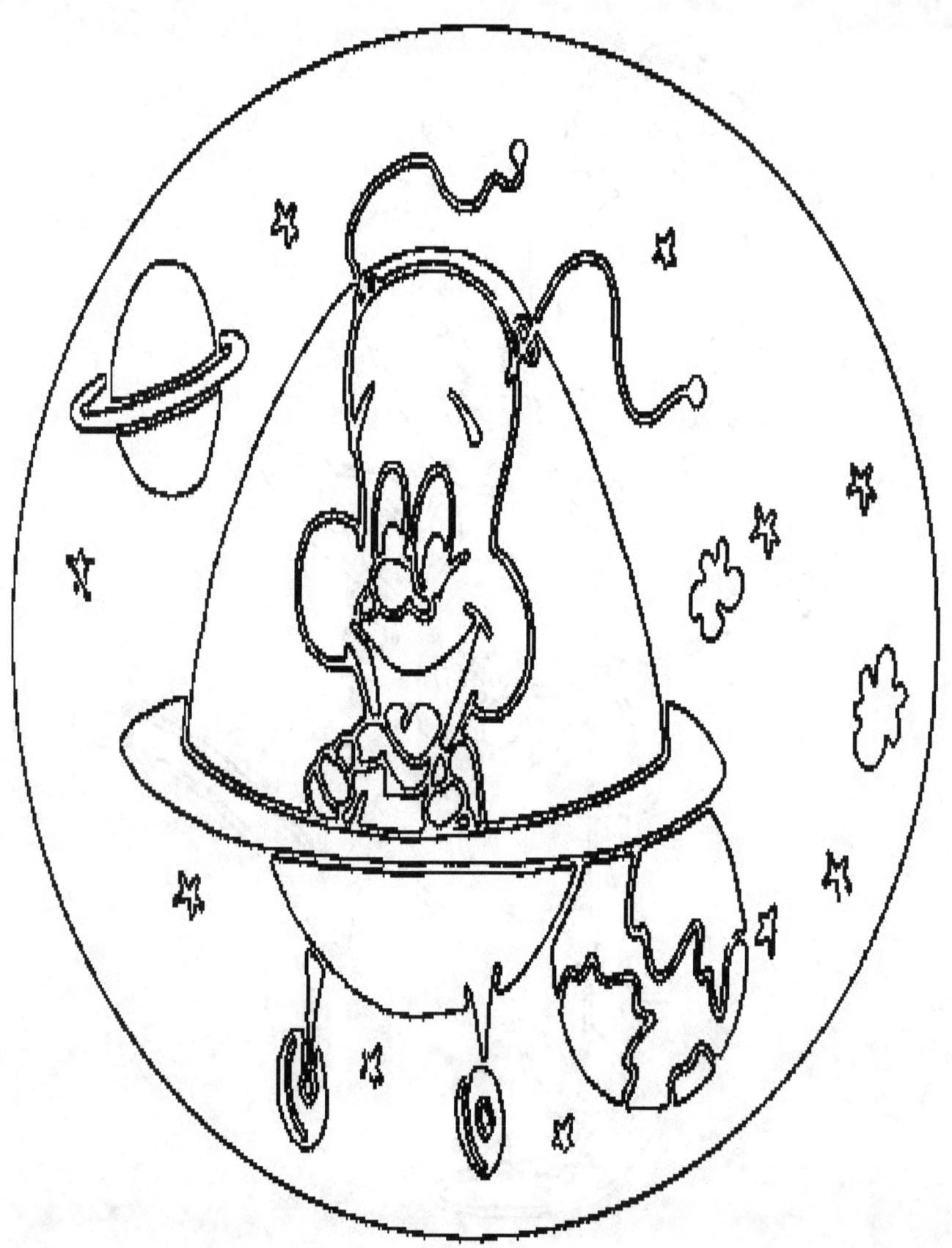

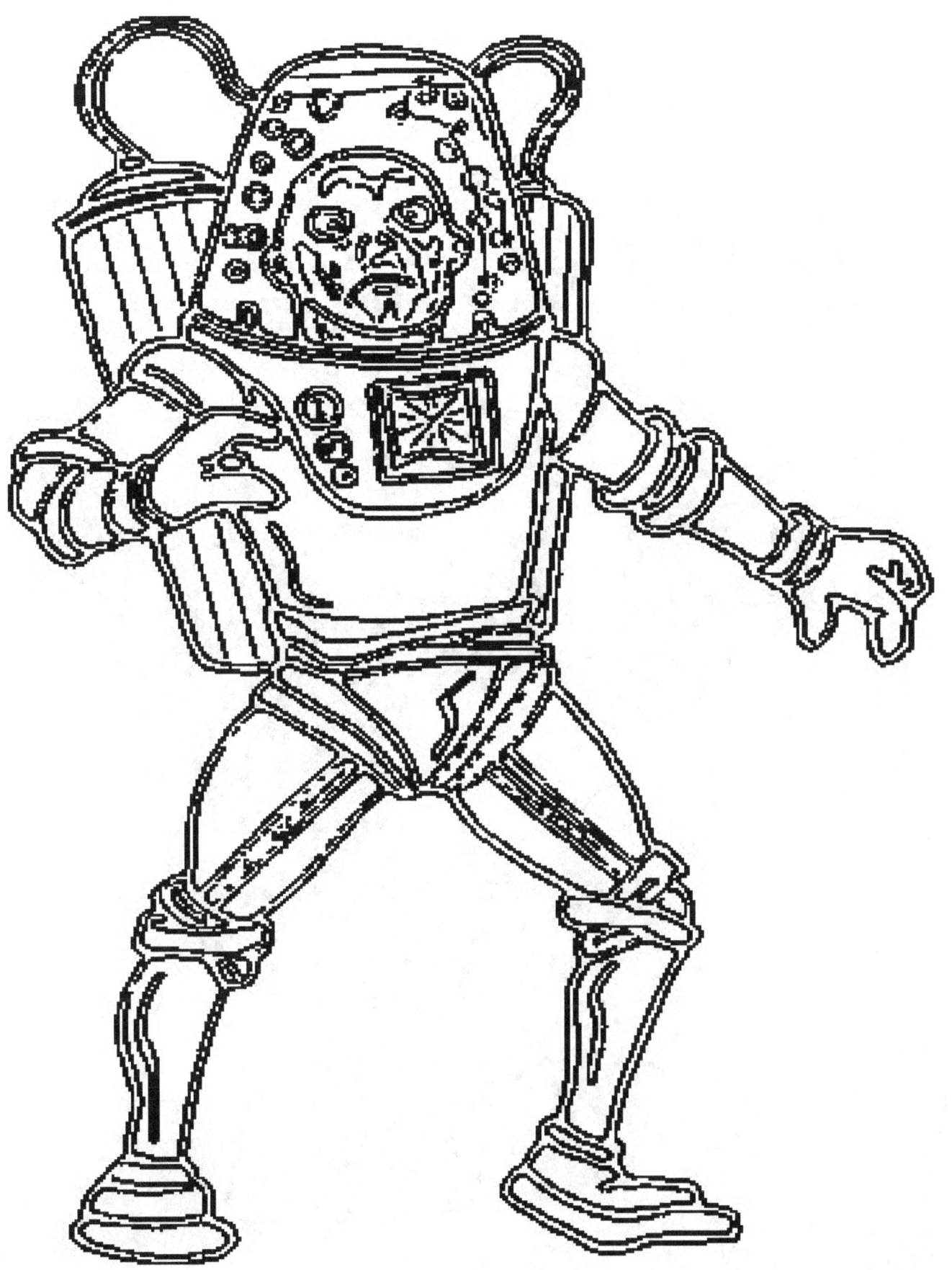

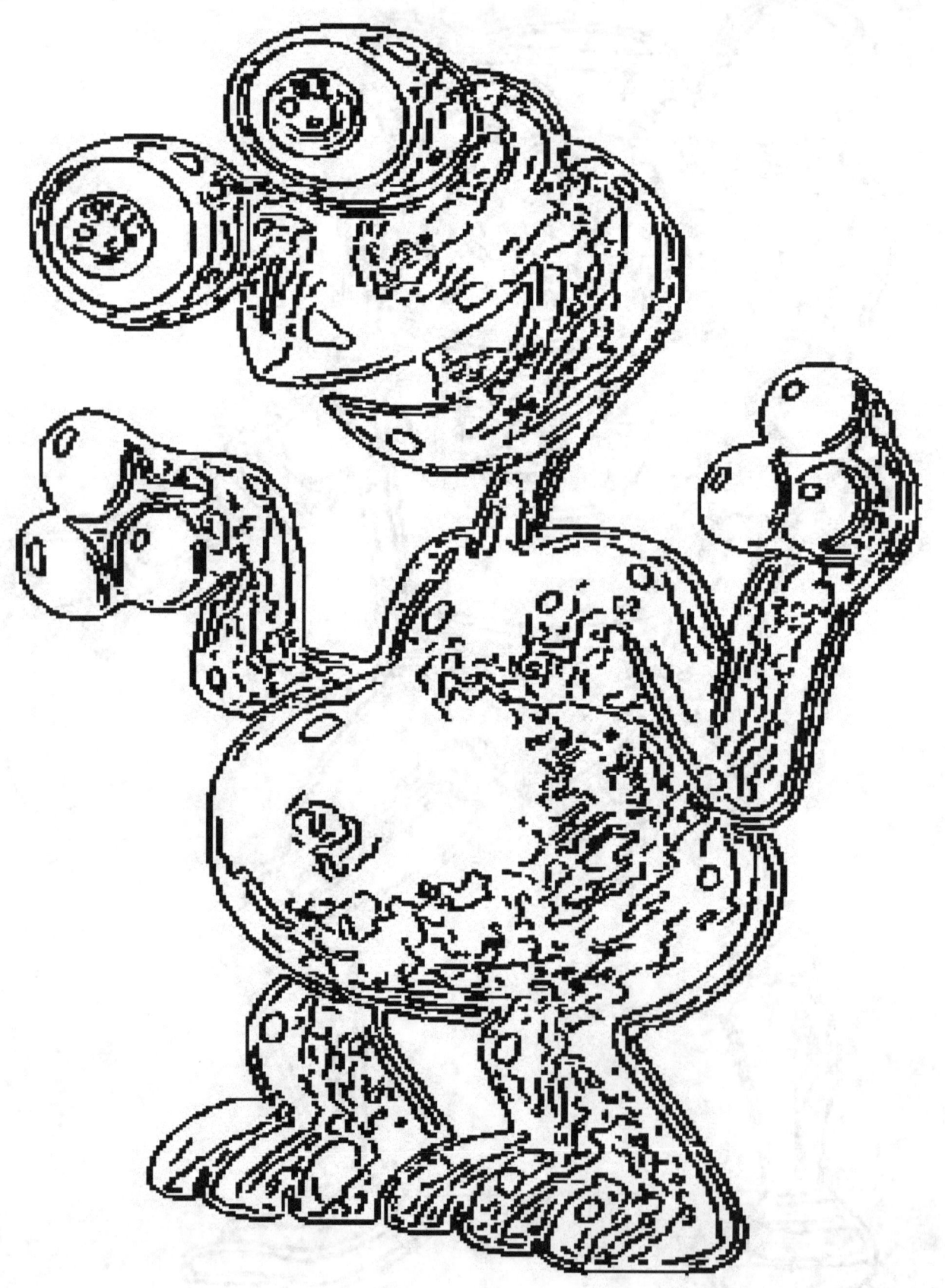

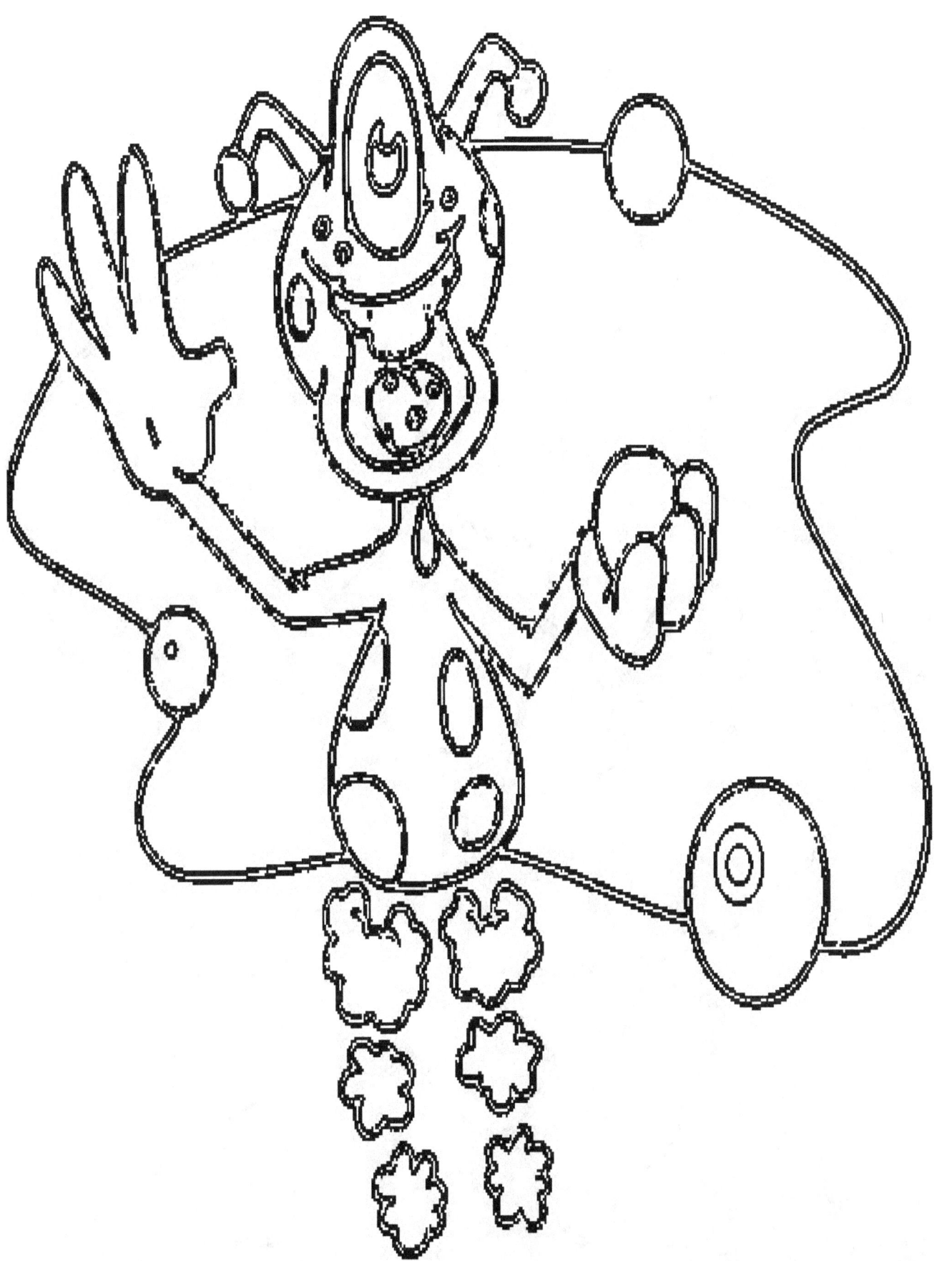

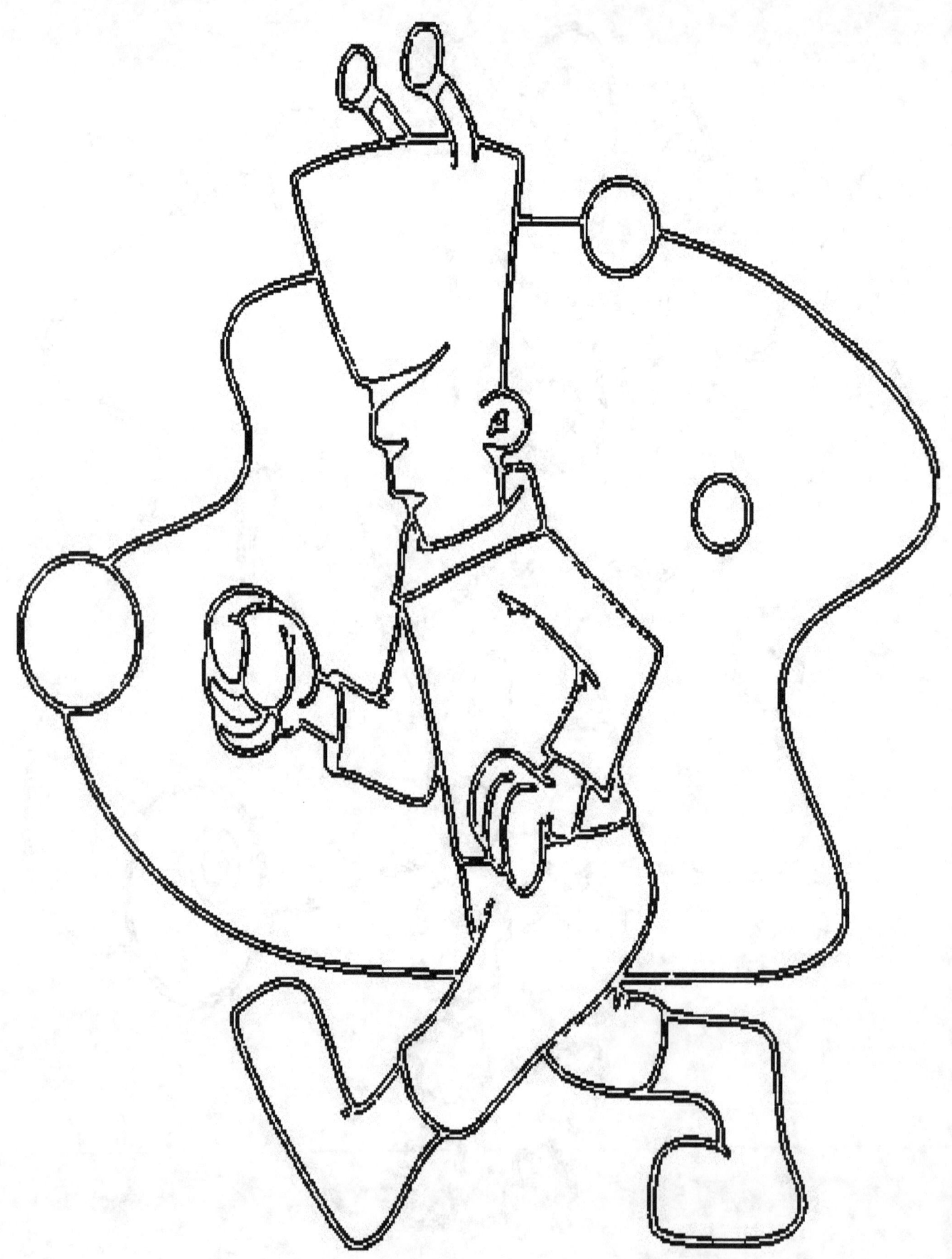

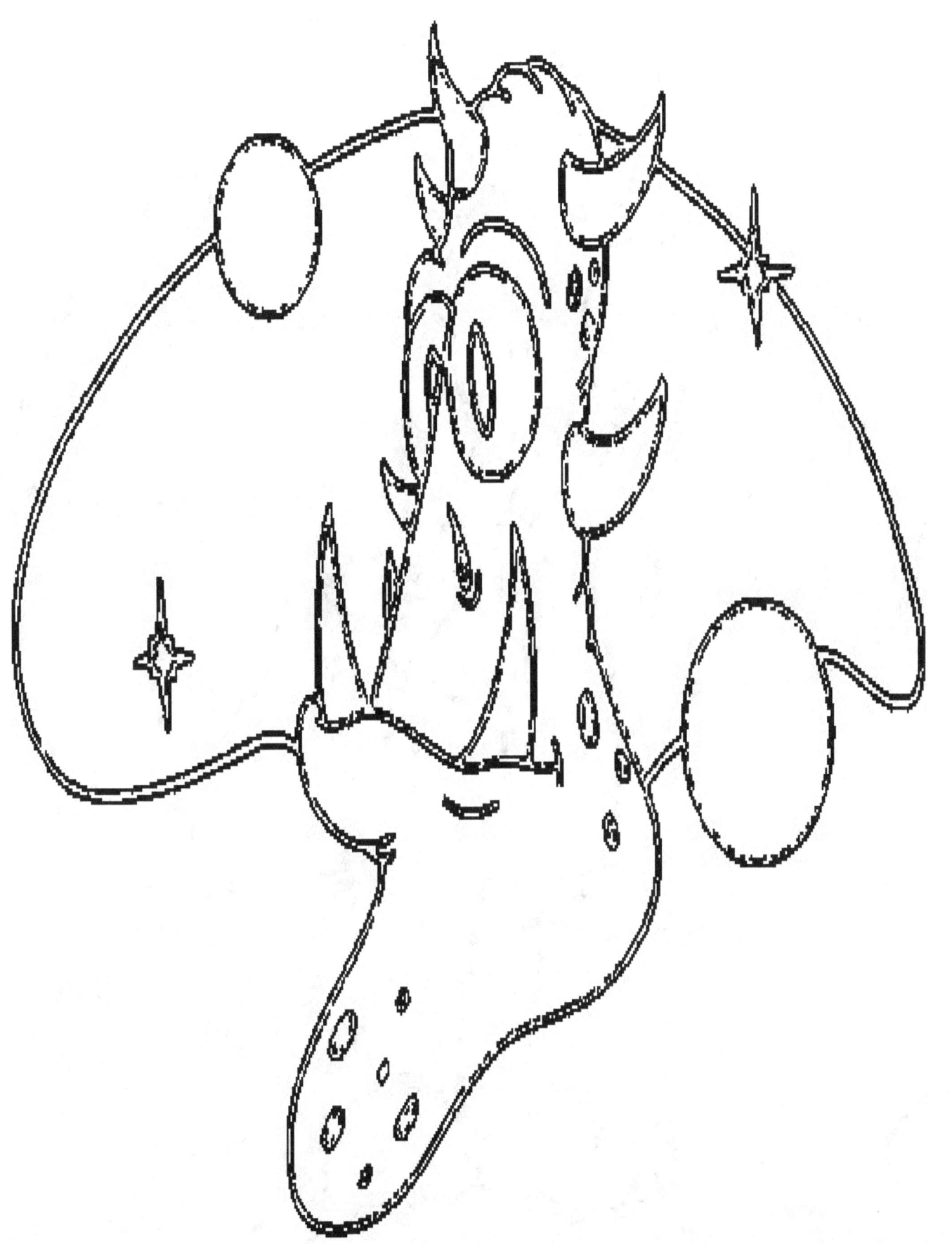

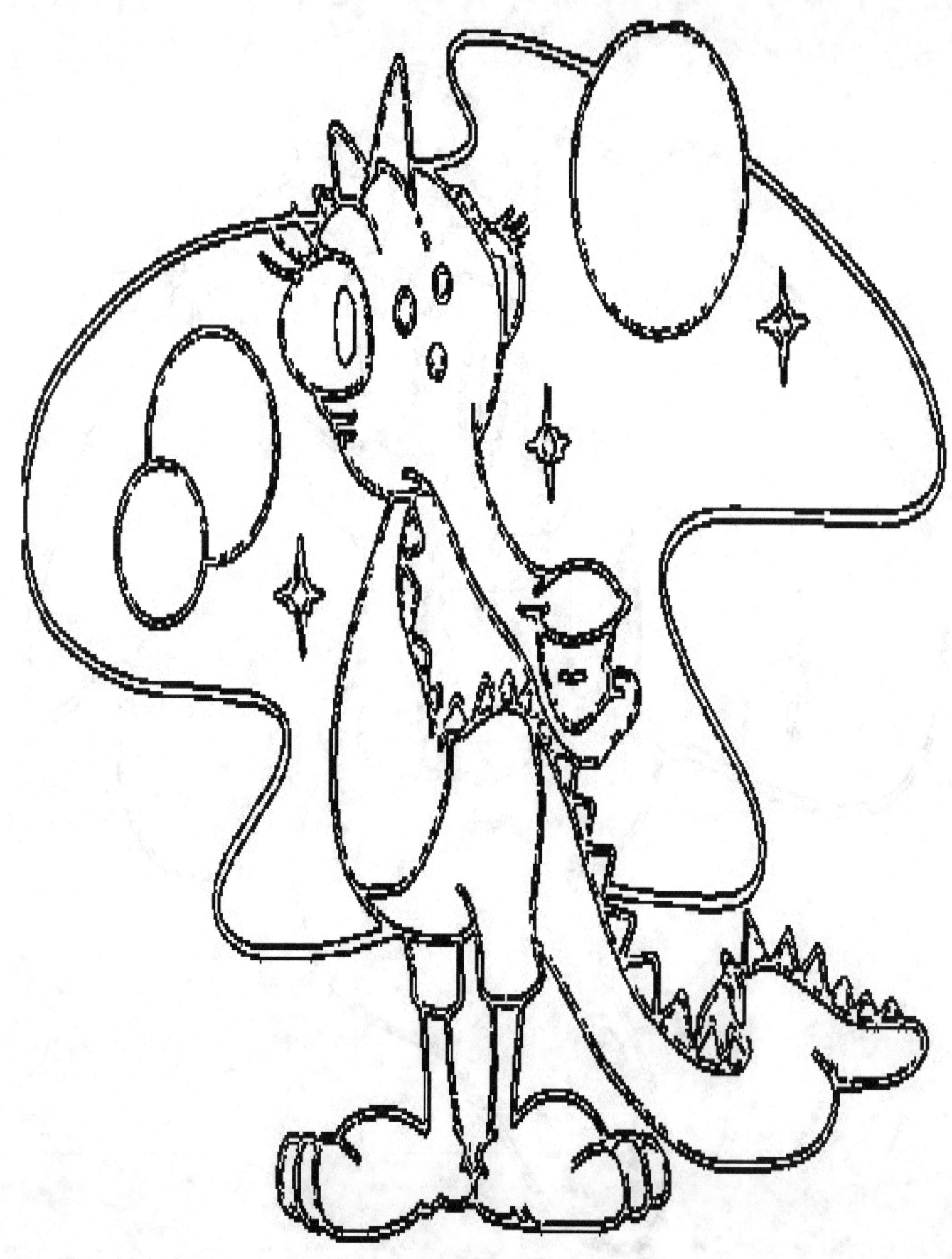

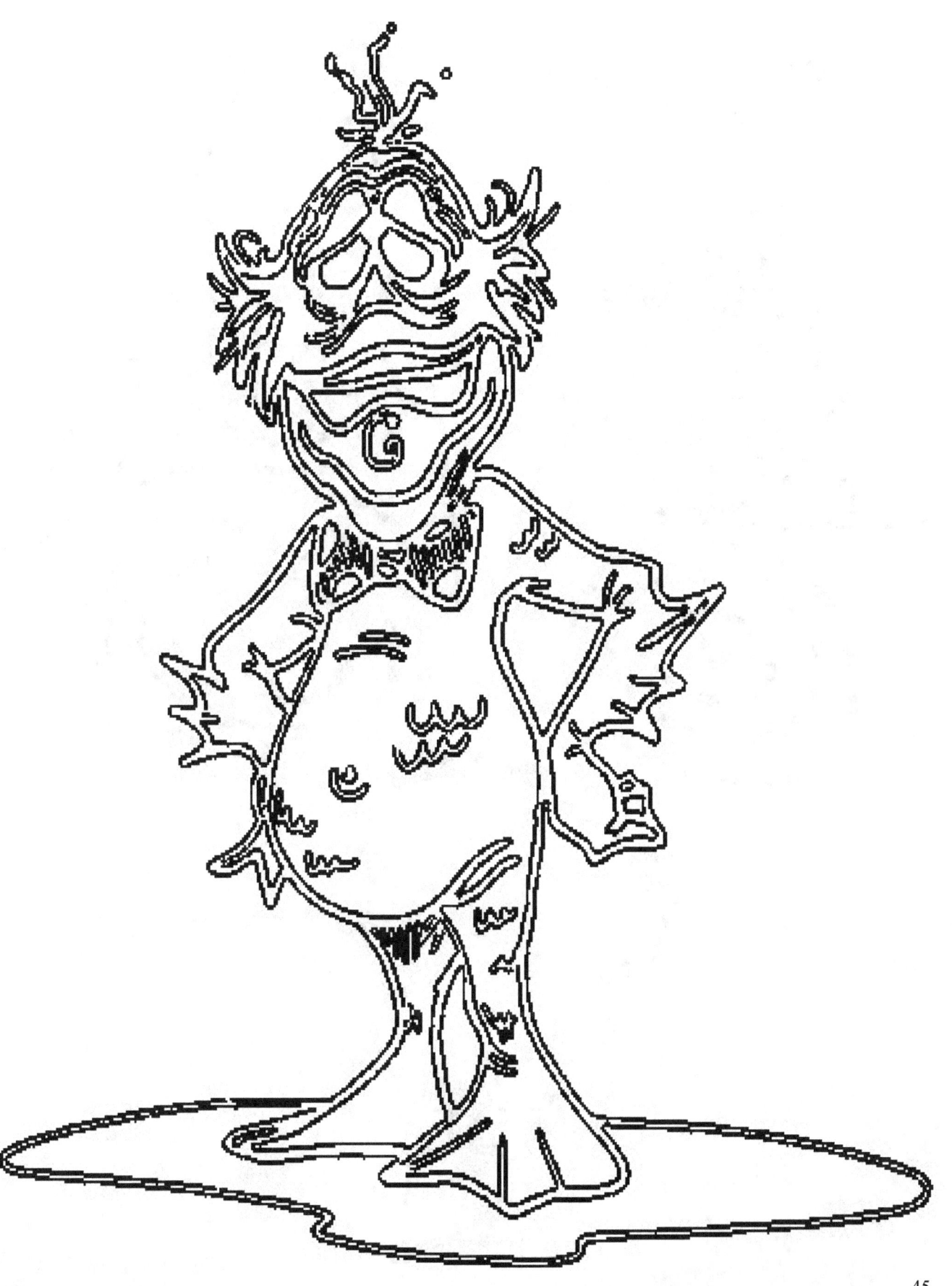

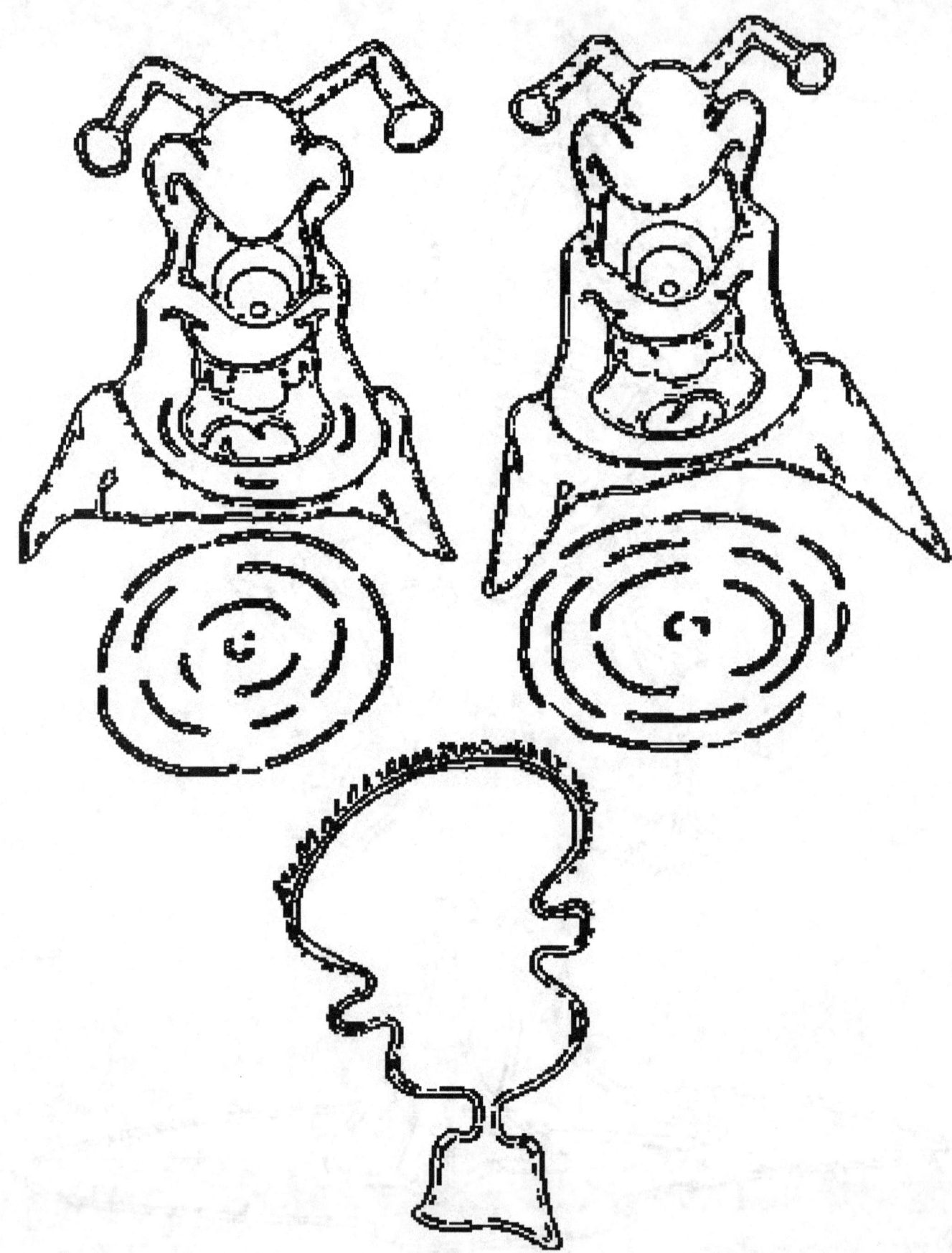

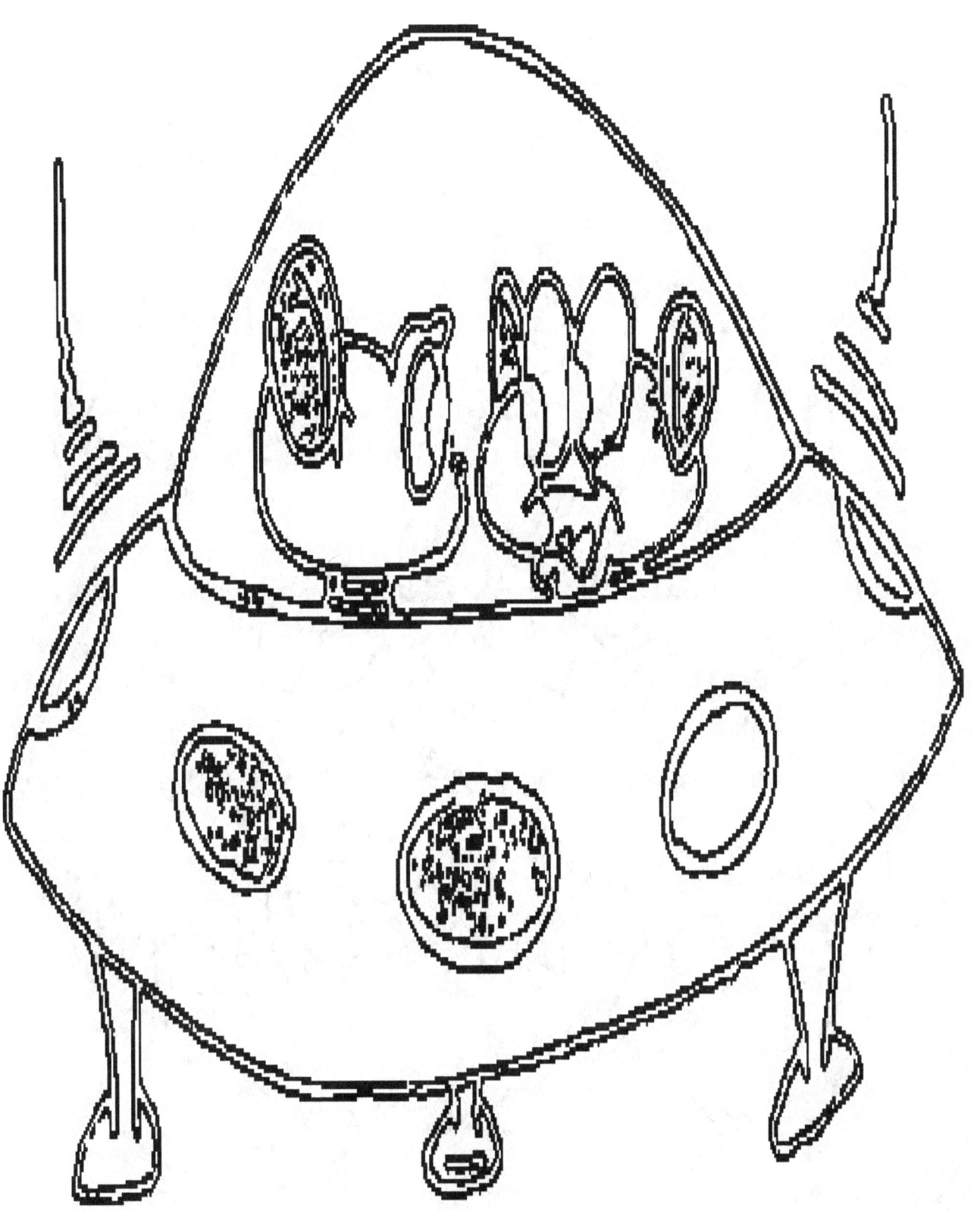

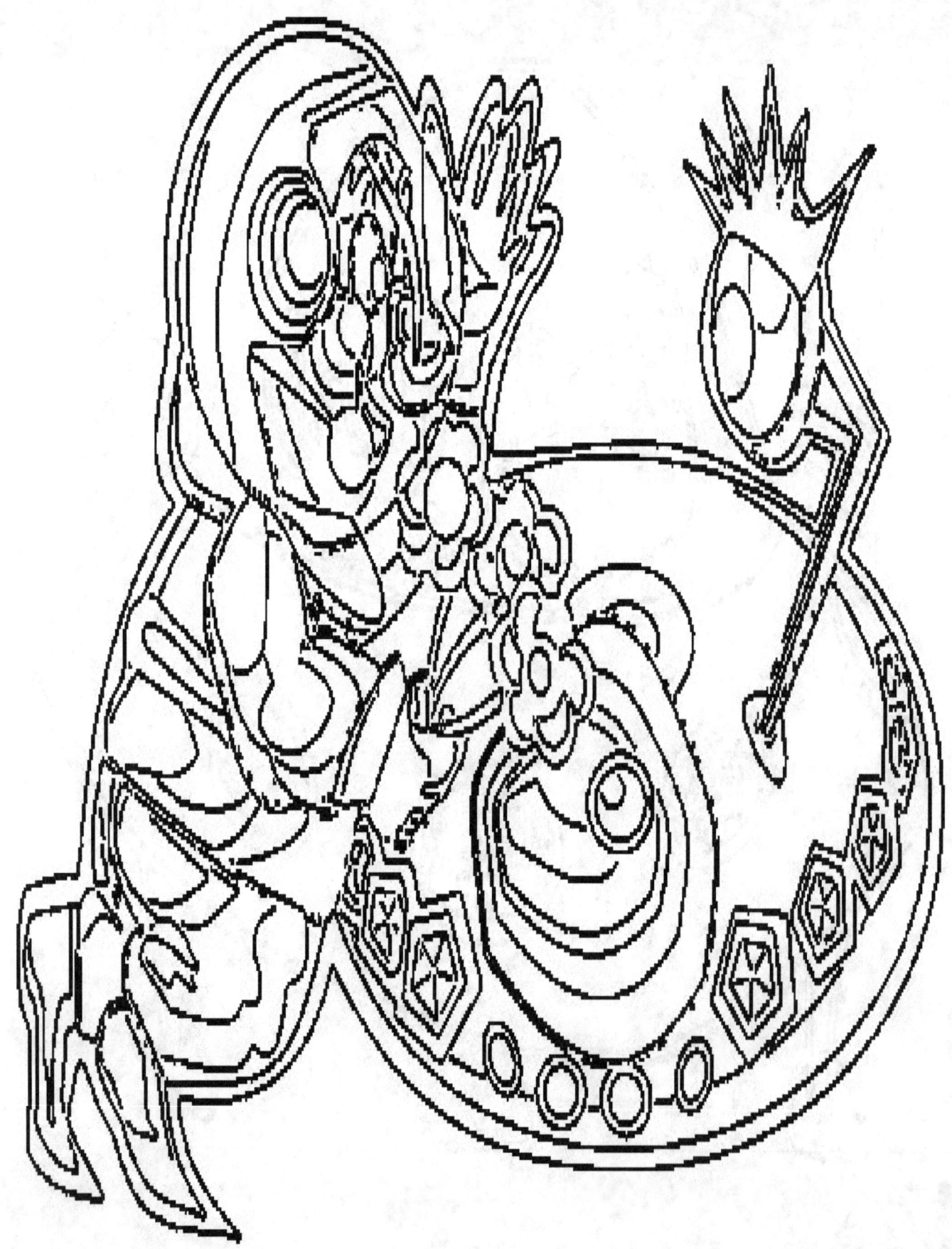

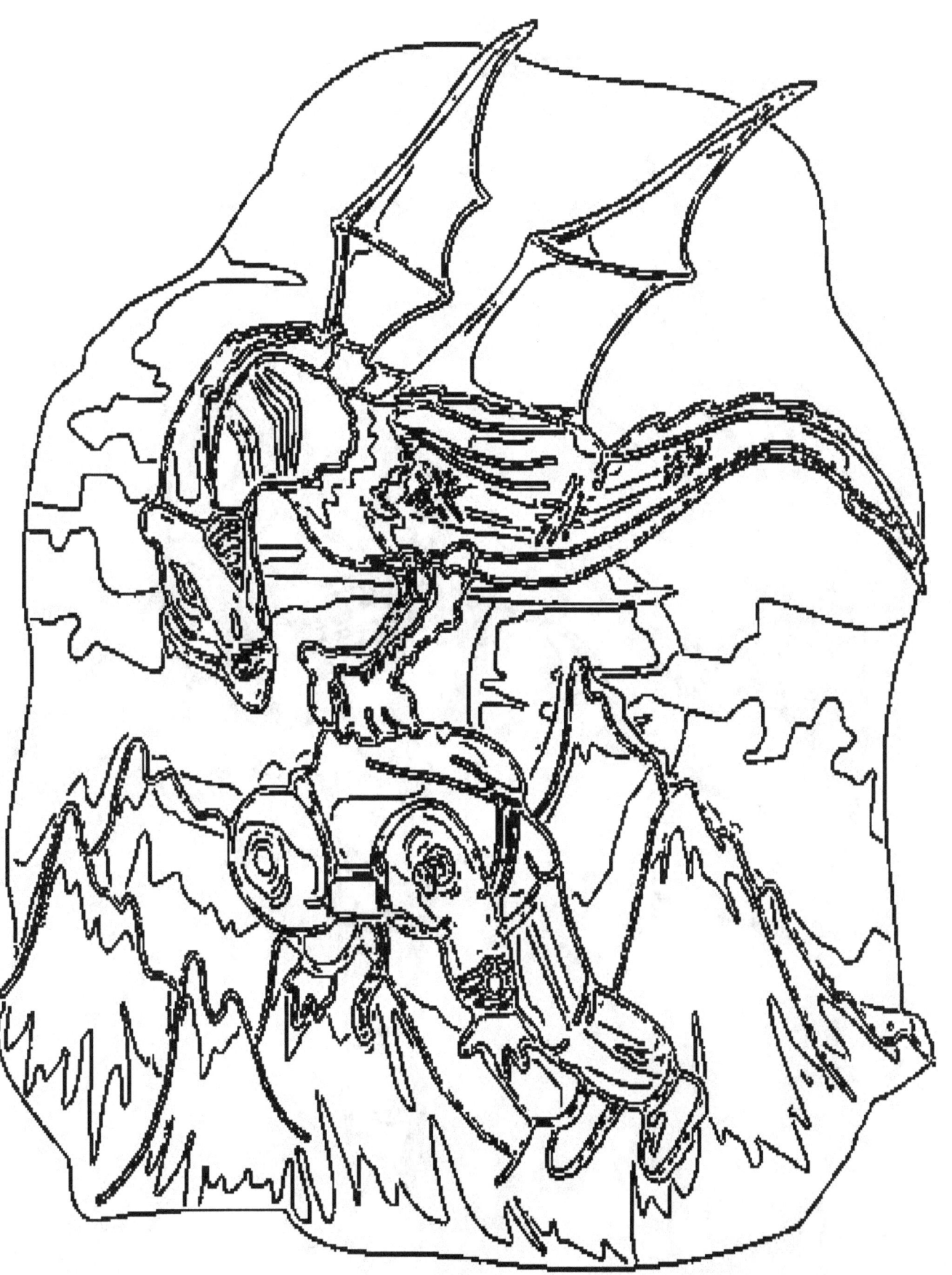

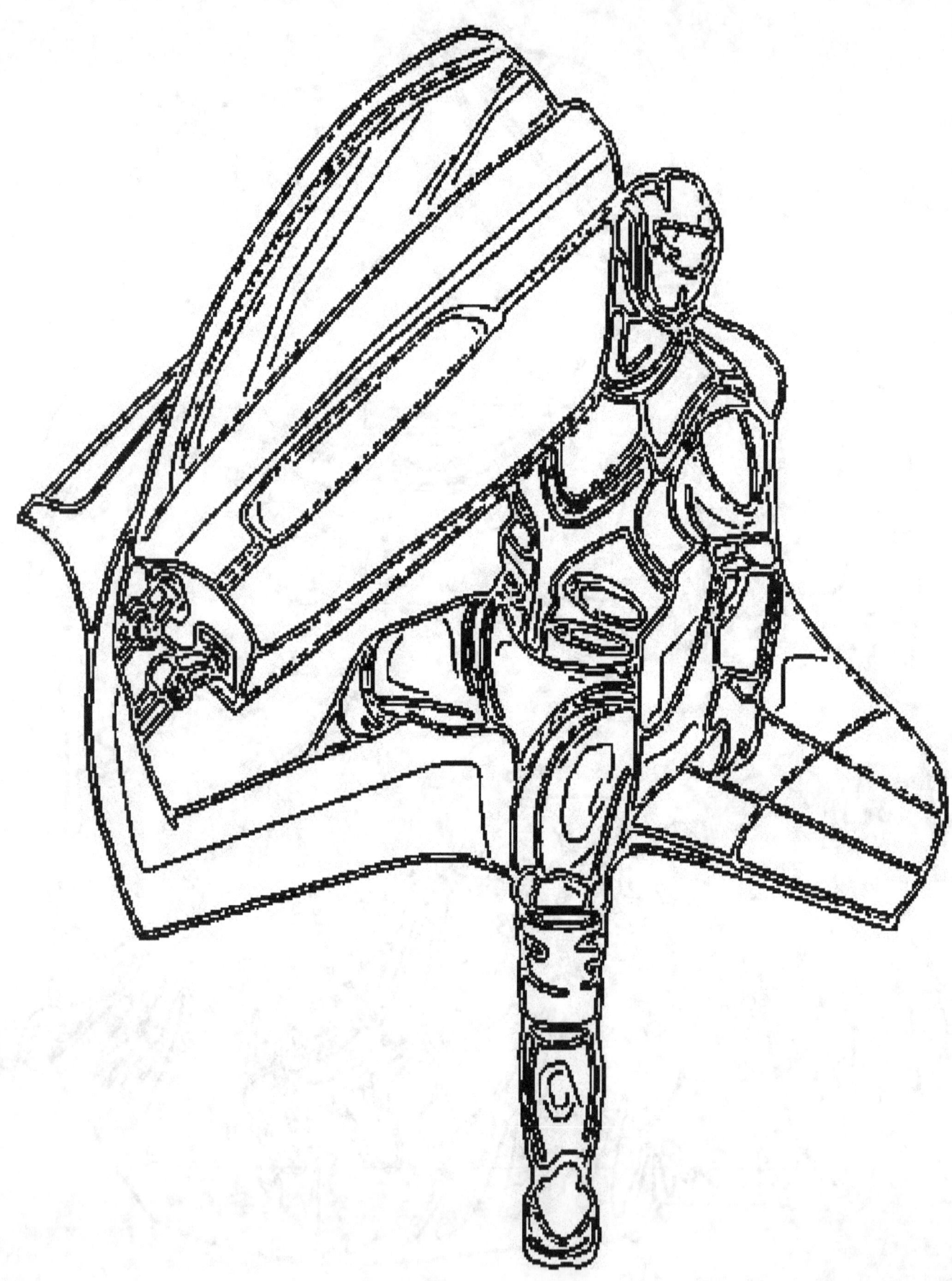

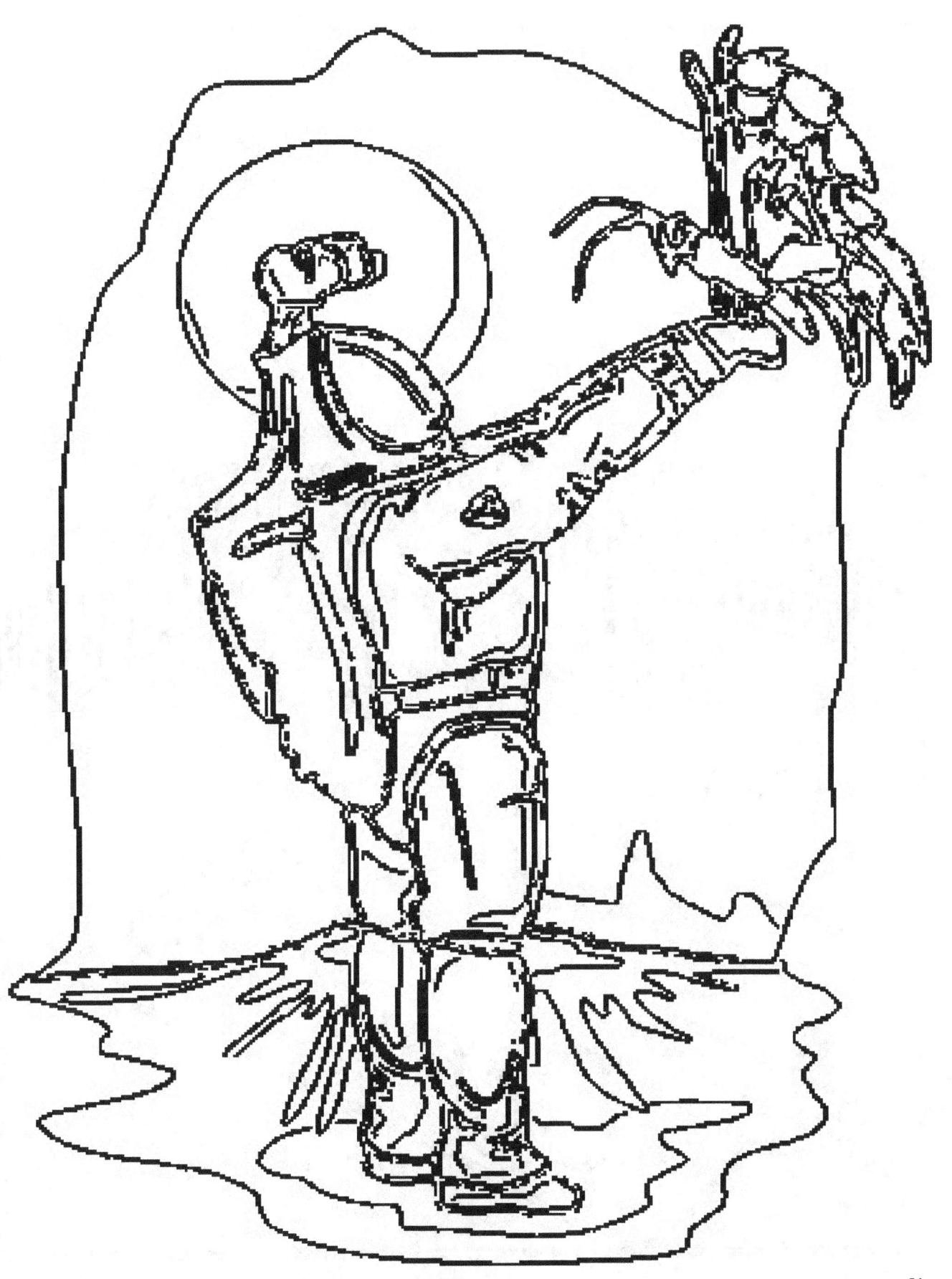

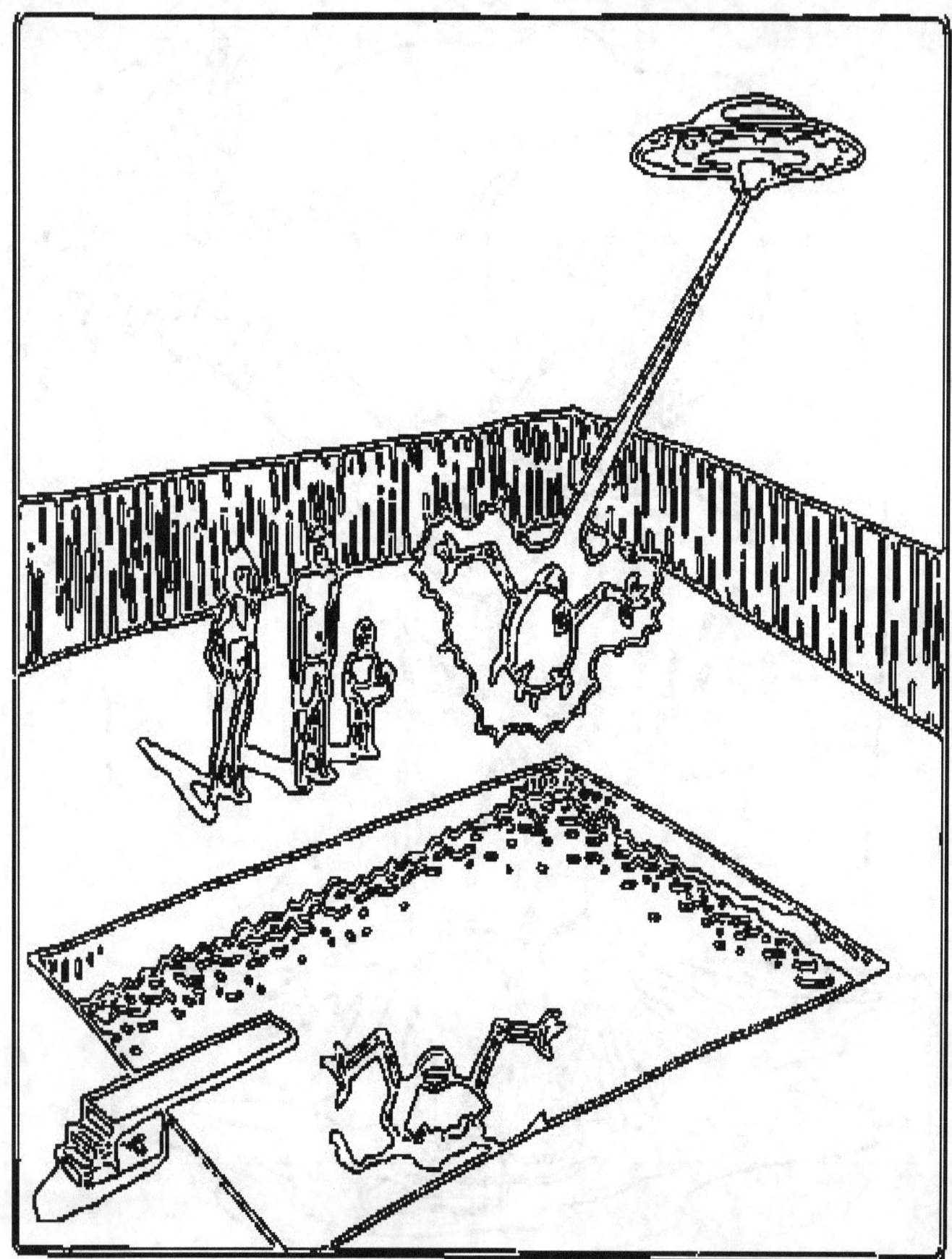

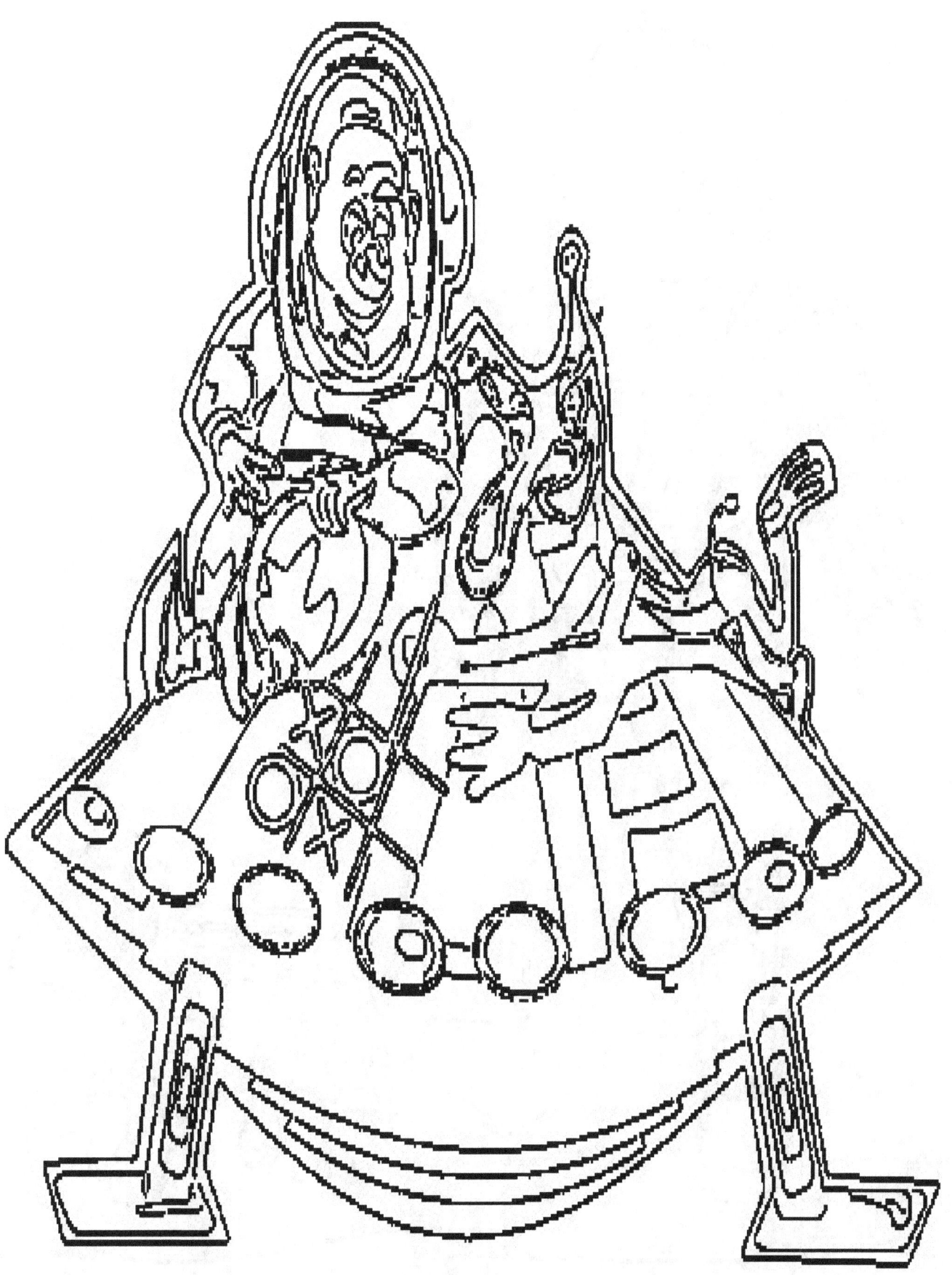

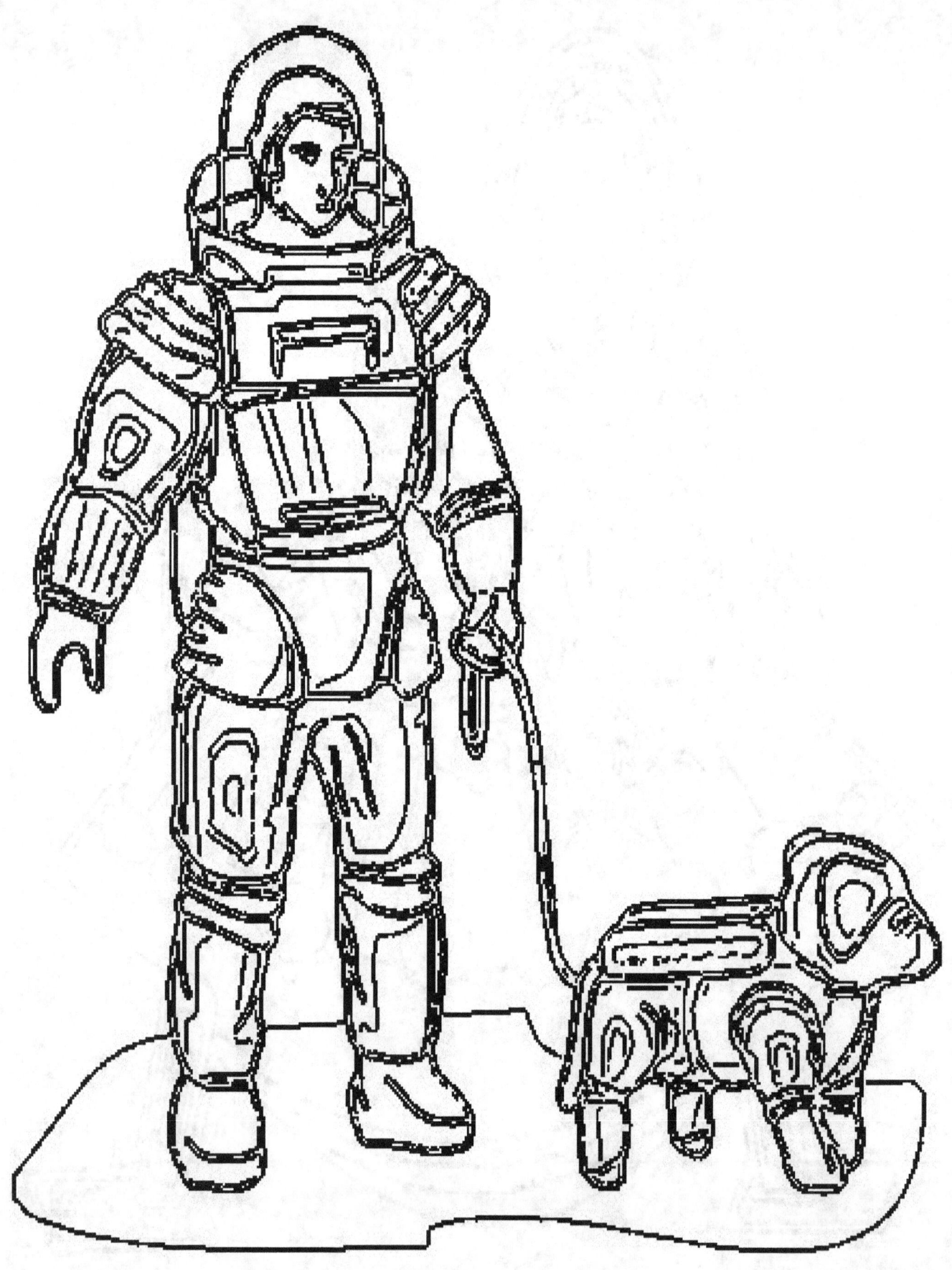

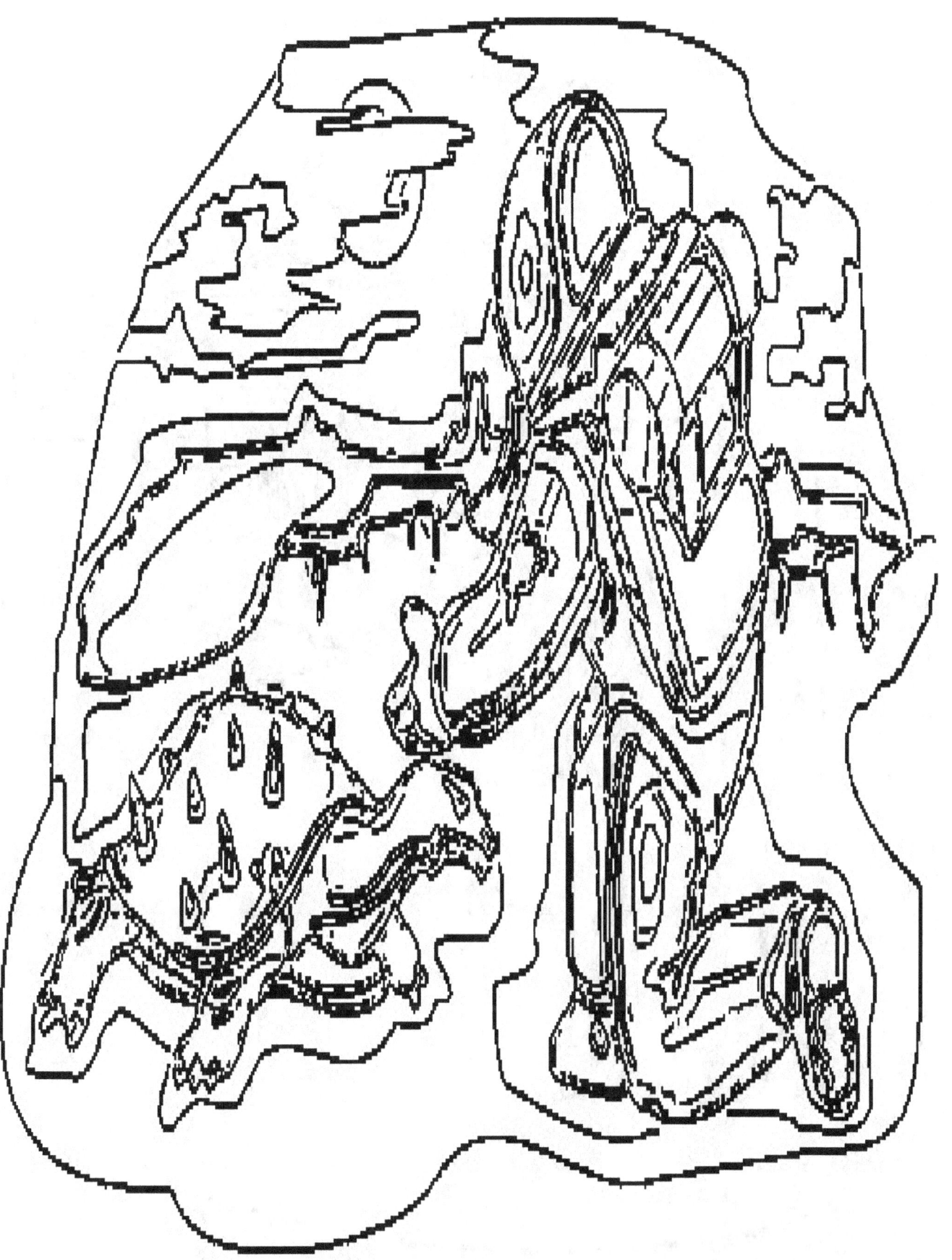

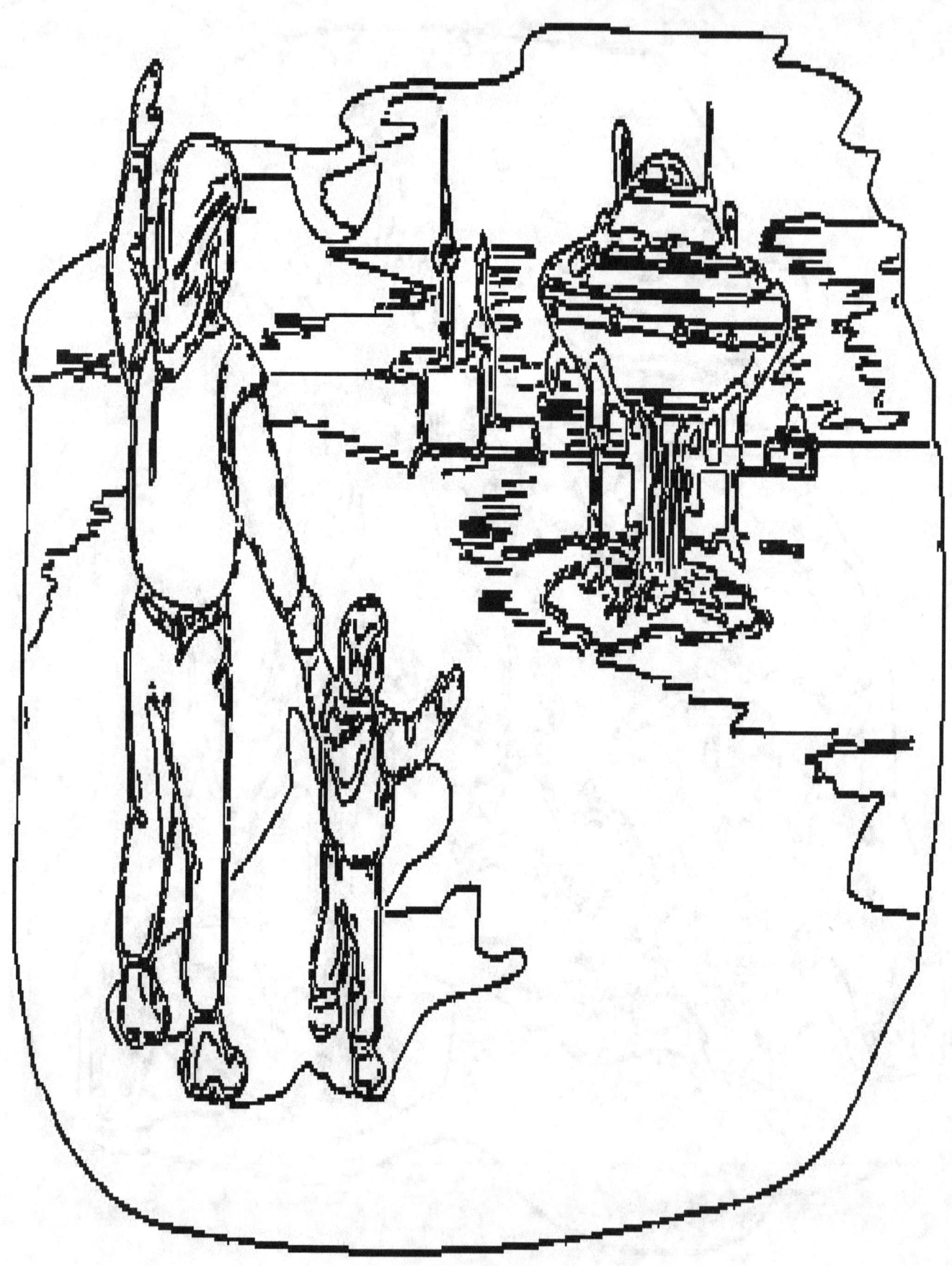

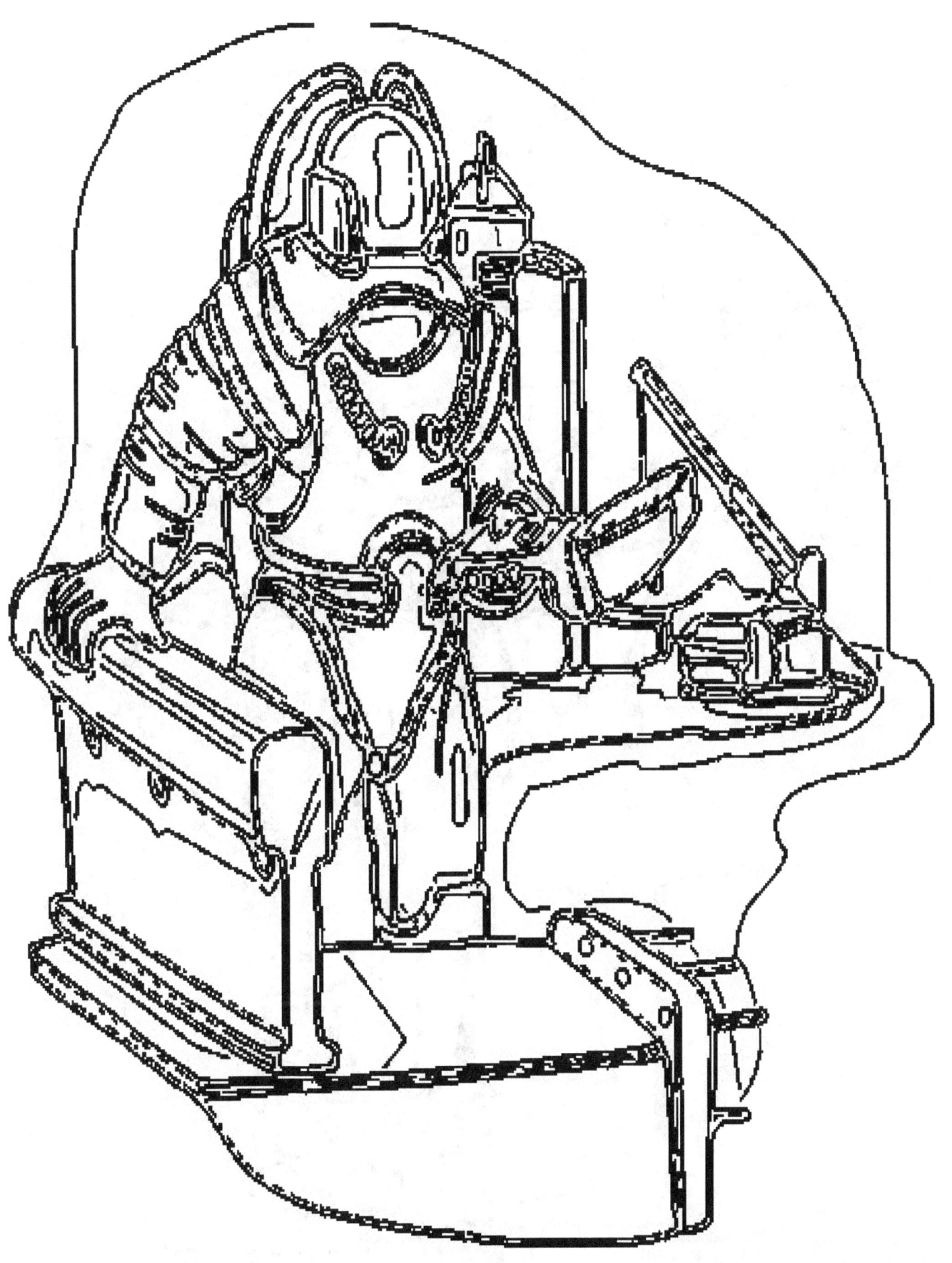

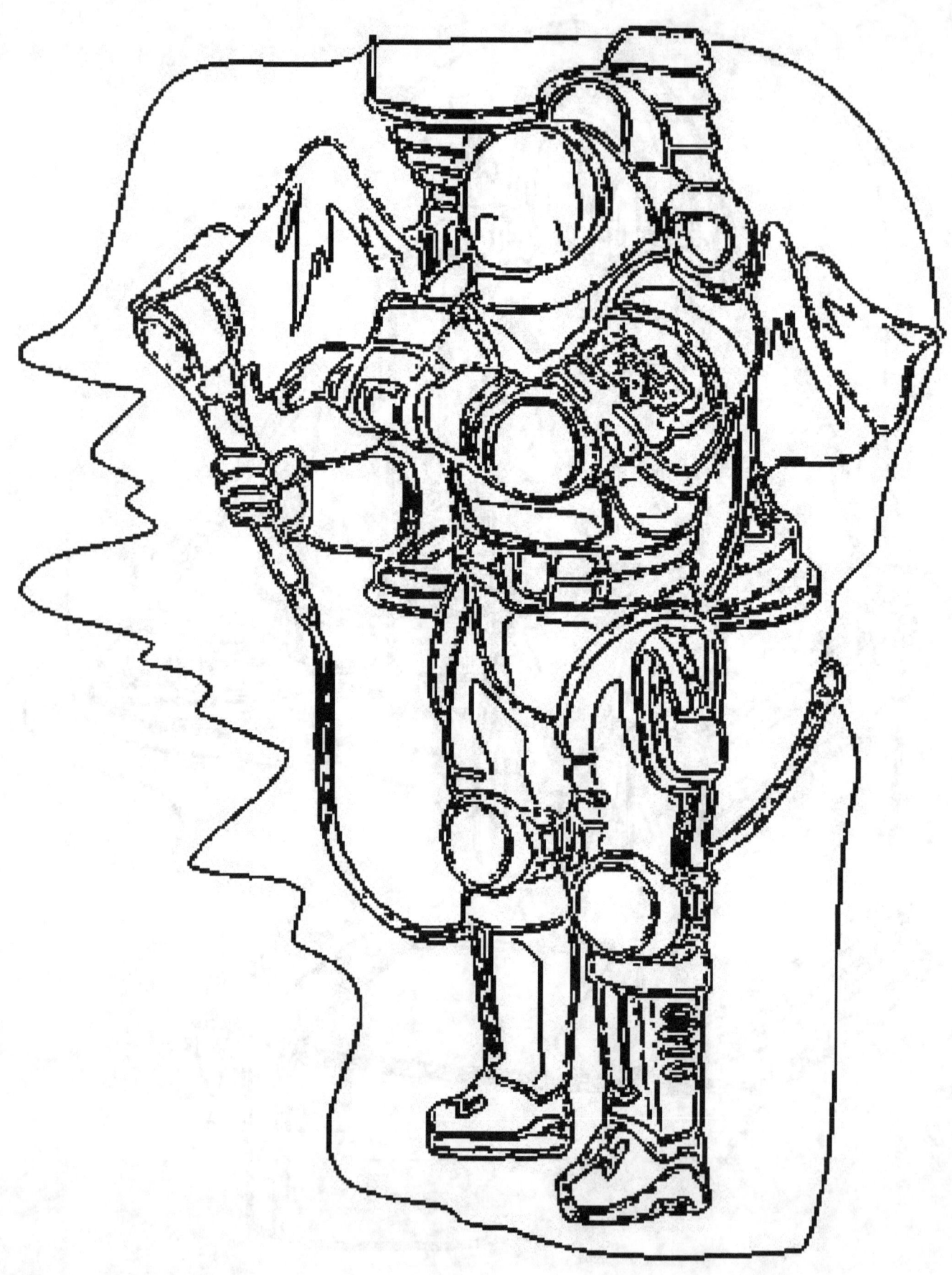

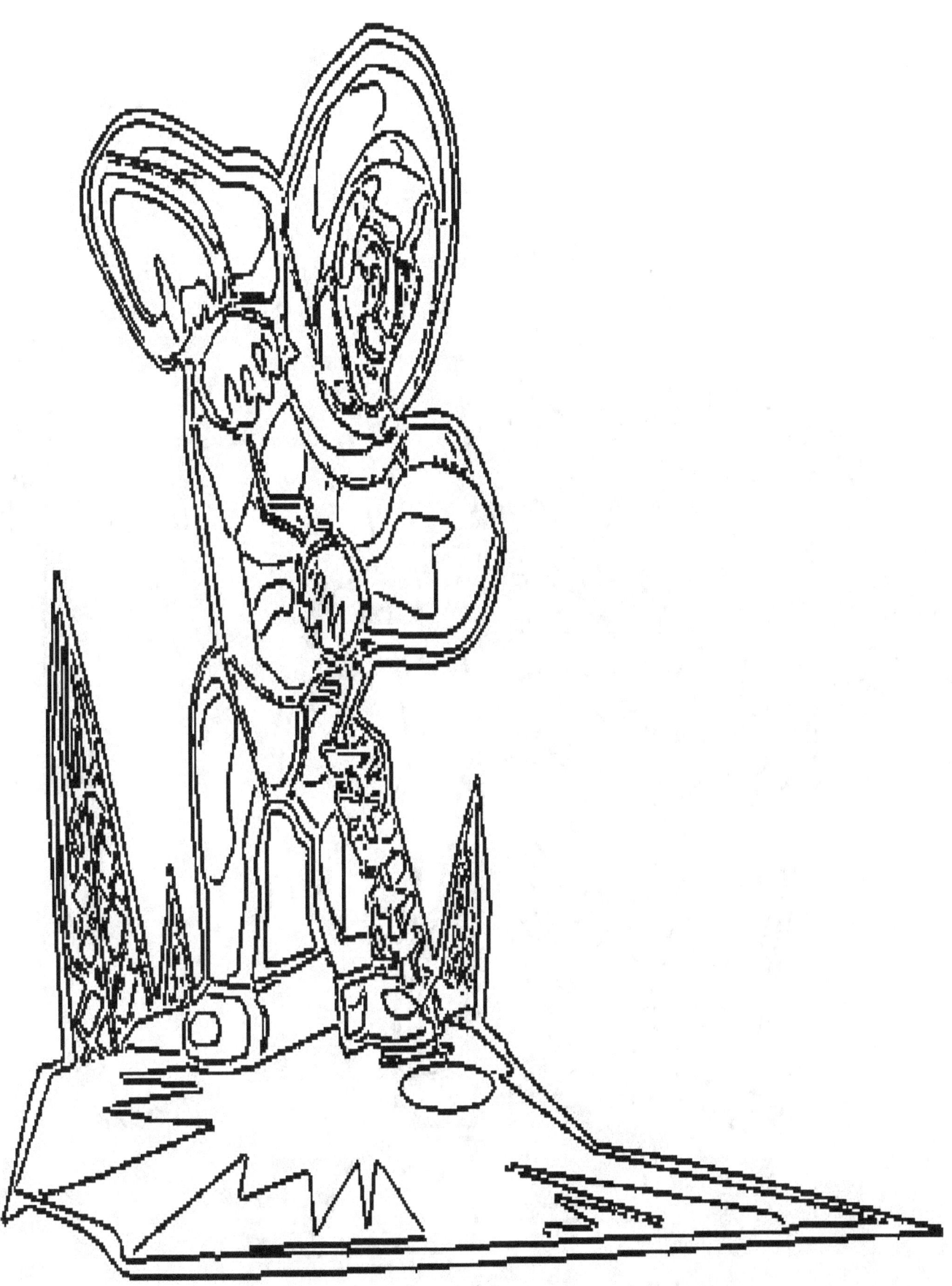

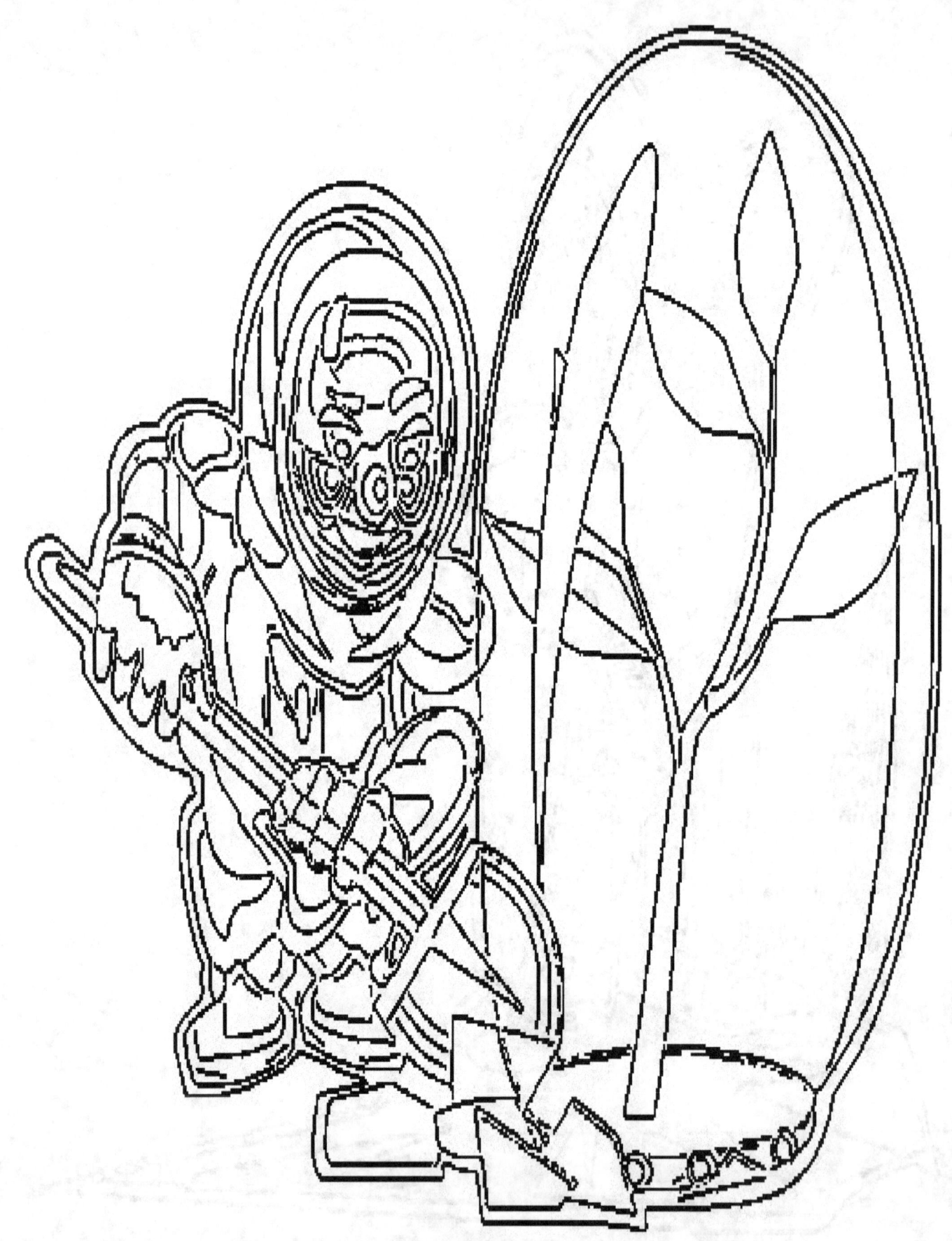

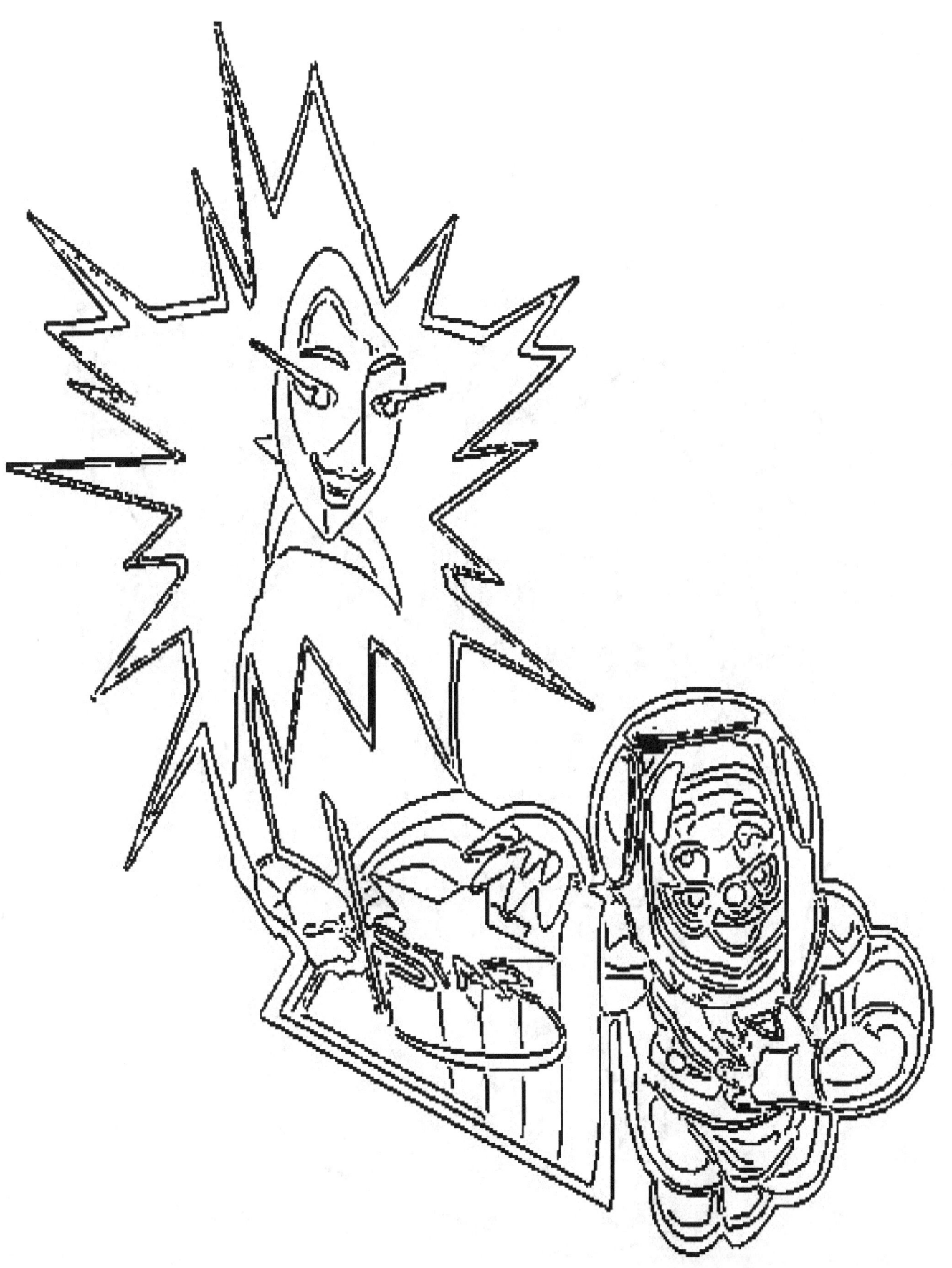

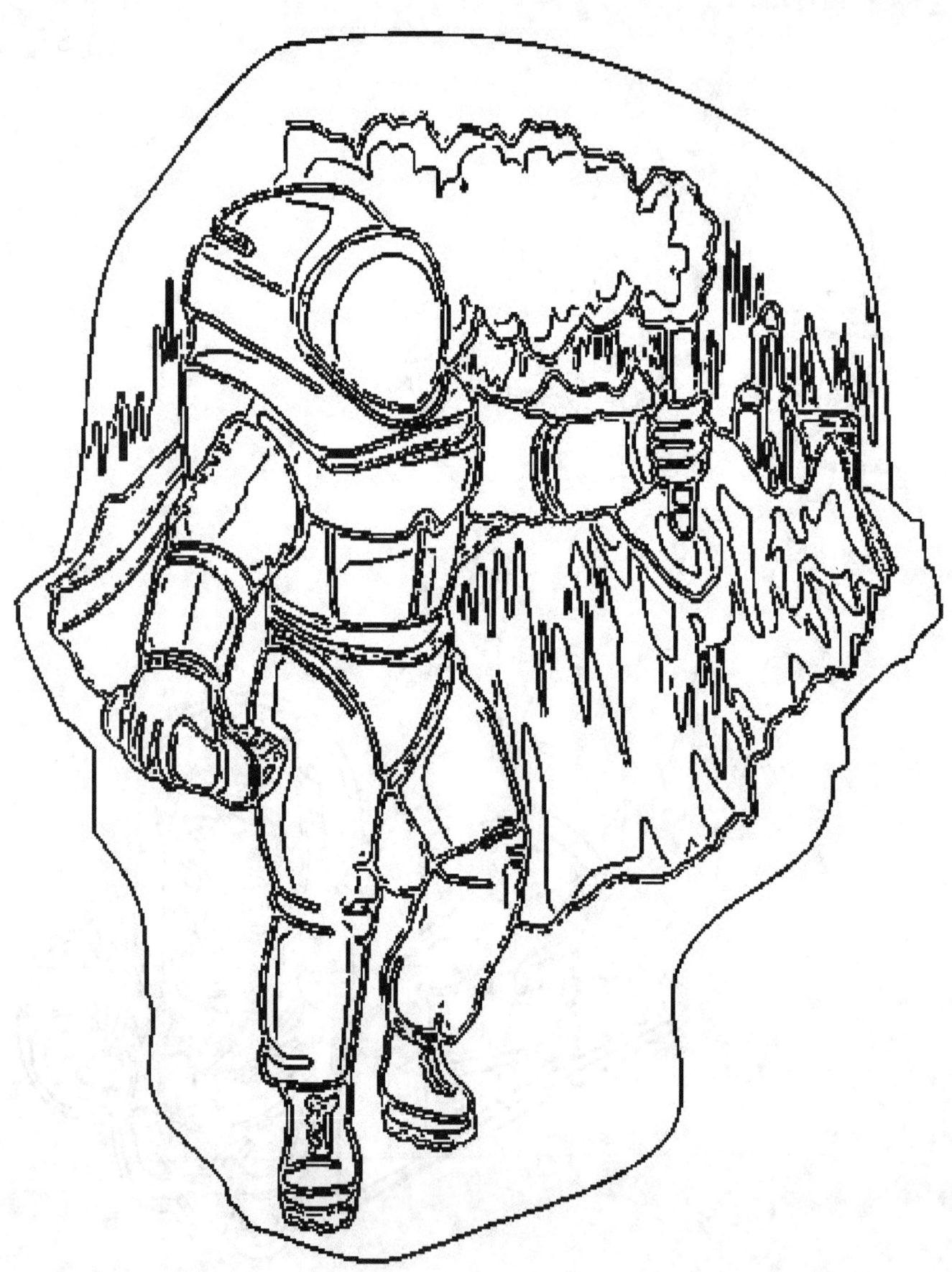

www.ingramcontent.com/pod-product-compliance
Lightning Source LLC
Chambersburg PA
CBHW081255180526
45170CB00007B/2432